REMOTE WORK
The new normal

Gren Gale

Copyright © Gren Gale 2020

The right to be identified as the author has been asserted by Gren Gale in accordance with the Copyright, Design and Patents Act 1988.

All rights reserved. No part of this publication may be reproduced, stored in a retrieval system or transmitted in any form or by any means, electronic, mechanical, photocopied, recorded or otherwise, without the prior permission of the author.

Cover image Avi Richards Unsplash

All cartoon images by Cartoon Resource - Shutterstock

A catalogue record for this book is recorded in the British Library.

ISBN 9798648912021

OTHER BOOKS BY GREN GALE

Project Management for SMEs

Project Management for SMBs (US version)

The Remote Project Manager

Thanks to all of the volunteer proof readers, particularly my wife for showing immense patience helping me turn some of my unreadable sentences into decent English.

CONTENTS

Foreword   8

1. Introduction

Why do you need this book?   12

2. Can you handle working remotely?

Introduction   16
The pluses and minuses of remote work   18
Finding remote work   30

3. How to build successful remote teams

Introduction   40
Teamwork   41
Communication   54
Respecting different cultures   68
Country specifics   79

4. Technology

Technology overview   83
Communication technology   87
Project and task management tools   102
Buying a task management or project management tool   111
Shared workspaces   130
Knowledge bases and Wikis   135

5. Security

The biggest issue	140
Technology	141
People	146
Remote access security audits	148

6. Legal Points

Contractual	152
Health and Safety	154
Discrimination	155
Bullying and Harassment	155
Confidential Information	156

7. Conclusion

It might even save the planet	160
Glossary	162
Index	166
Credits/Notes	172

Foreword

Around 15 years ago, I ran a home working pilot for a major company. Office space was tight and it was one of the alternatives investigated to continue to achieve our objectives without increasing office rental bills. Line speeds were poor and broadband expensive, so some employees taking part in the pilot were using dial-up. Almost no applications existed to facilitate working from home. Videoconferencing over the internet was unheard of and most people worked off-line and then connected every hour or so to synchronise e-mails and documents with the servers at head office. The pilot was carried out with around 30 volunteers working one day a week at home over three months. For the employees it was an unqualified success. They loved being freed from the grind of the commute, most started work earlier and finished later but loved the opportunity to work with fewer interruptions and get on top of their week's work. Many who usually spent their working week meeting-bound re-organised their calendars to take meetings for four days and do their desk work at home. As a result they felt more satisfied and more productive. The only issue expressed was a concern about weight gain with the kitchen a little too close for comfort! Sadly when I reported the results to the company's board the senior management were unimpressed. They had concerns about disempowerment of managers who might not be able to track employees down, control and measurement of the tasks that employees were carrying out, arranging meetings with people who were out of the office and trust that people were actually working and not watching TV all day.

Things have moved incredibly fast in the intervening years. Broadband speeds have increased dramatically and a wealth of tools are available that plug the confidence gaps expressed by that board of directors. Videoconferencing, instant messaging, task and project management tools, shared storage, knowledge bases as well as email have all increased the ability to contact, involve, manage and motivate employees working remotely.

As line speeds have increased and more tools become available, so has the prevalence of home working with many companies embracing remote working as the way they see office work evolving. However progress was gradual and evolutionary until world events caused a switch from evolution to revolution. I began writing this book early in 2020 and completed it in the middle of the COVID-19 epidemic when home working well and truly came into its own. Firms who could, sent their employees home with their laptops and in most cases expanded existing infrastructure to take the extra load. Zoom witnessed 1000% increase in users with Slack and Microsoft Teams also seeing massive increases in paying customers. All of these new users witnessed the potential and viability of remote working. Despite the far from ideal circumstances, hundreds of millions have enjoyed the experience of home working and become comfortable with the technology. Remote working is here to stay.

My own history with remote working goes back a long way. From that pilot in 2005 I've managed countless teams and projects based all over the world with me as the office based co-ordinator. However I took it a step further in 2013 when I left the office behind and began working remotely. I've barely set foot in an office since! So while the COVID-19 lockdown had little effect on my working life, by curtailing my social life it gave a real boost to my efforts to complete this book. While a lot of research as well as hands-on experience has gone into this book, I was suddenly able to tap into a rich vein of articles from people in lockdown describing individual experiences of working from home.

Here's how this book is laid out. **Chapter 1 is the introduction** and lets you know why you might find this book useful. **Chapter 2 asks if remote working is right for you,** looks at the pluses and minuses of working remotely, lets you know what types of jobs are going remote, where to find remote work and how to pass a remote interview. **Chapter 3 asks how can you build successful remote teams** and looks at how to build teamwork, how to organise remote teams, meet-ups and hackathons, remote social events, how to adapt how you communicate to working remotely, addresses the challenges in building teams with a mix of cultures and languages and then looks at country specific issues like differing working weeks and time zones. **Chapter 4 is about the choosing the right technology** to support remote work from the huge number of vendors and packages available. It covers videoconferencing software, instant messaging, e-mail, project and task management packages including workflow, shared workspaces and co-authoring, knowledge bases and wikis. It covers the major vendors and what features you should look for. **Chapter 5 covers security** – arguably the biggest issue with remote working. **Chapter 6 addresses the legal considerations** with remote working from contractual, health and safety, to potential claims of discrimination, harassment and cyber-bullying. I hope you enjoy reading the book as much as I've enjoyed writing it.

As you can see from my bibliography I have another book in print called **The Remote Project Manager**. That and this book share a lot of common material so I wouldn't suggest you buy both.

1
INTRODUCTION

Why do you need this book?

Offices packed with rows of desks and crowded contact centres are destined to become quaint images of the past. Remote work has come of age and is about to become the new normal.

While for many years now it's been no secret that lots of office based jobs could be carried out remotely, the COVID-19 crisis turned that potential into reality for many businesses worldwide. Offices full of endless rows of desks and packed contact centres are likely to become distant memories of a past era as people move away from office to home based work in ever increasing numbers. To paraphrase just about every politician and journalist commentating during the COVID-19 pandemic, remote working looks like becoming the 'new normal'.

More than that with millions of households in lockdown necessity proved to be the mother of invention and many businesses and social institutions moved their operations into 'remote' mode. Schools, colleges and universities made full use of technology already rolled out to students but previously only sparingly utilised. Classes in everything from languages to fitness and health started to build viable revenue models based on the use of videoconferencing and other collaboration applications. Medical practitioners from family doctors to physiotherapists started offering remote diagnosis and treatment. Deprived of physical proximity the use of individual videoconferencing went through the roof.

The Economist in 2020 estimated that in the UK 44% of jobs could be carried out from home while in the US the figure was 42%[15]. These numbers are only likely to grow.

The technology to support remote work has not only existed but laid dormant or barely used in many institutions. The COVID-19 pandemic provided the impetus and funding that has fed a boom in slick and innovative technologies to support remote work. With fast internet becoming almost universally accessible and the technology to support working remotely mushrooming it has become very easy for many businesses to go remote and have teams located in multiple locations.

The attraction of remote work for a wide range of institutions and enterprises is immense. Office costs can be slashed and scarce talent recruited from all over the world without the hassle of having to obtain work permits and immigration clearance. Employees like it. Studies have found that employees tend to be happier and more productive working from home[16] and value the improvement in their work-life balance. It also provides built in resilience. As the COVID-19 pandemic proved remote working is a strong weapon in disaster preparedness and recovery.

While the impetus was unfortunate, the consequences of the pandemic are likely to be transformational. Running teams remotely has always required a leap of faith with many companies wary of putting much more than a toe in the water. Forced to choose between home-working or no working, companies organised quickly around the new reality of remote work. However in most cases existing ways of working were left unaltered other than the introduction of videoconferencing. Fighting a new war with the approach used to win the last one is a continuing theme. Companies need to reorganise, devise new approaches and adopt more and better collaboration technology to ensure remote working really works.

So what will this book do for you? We'll let you know how to overcome the difficulties and challenges that present themselves both to individuals who work remotely and to companies wanting to build effective and productive remote teams. There is an ever expanding suite of tools available that can supercharge remote working. Videoconferencing is the key technology but you'll also want to share data, manage and organise work, message, e-mail and enforce security. We'll help you find your way through the bewilderment of technology available from literally hundreds of vendors and how to make best use of it. We'll also help you determine how you can work effectively and sensitively with individuals and teams who could be located anywhere in the world and deal with potential language and cultural differences. Companies need also to be cognisant of Health and Safety, security, legal and discrimination issues that may come out of remote working.

As an individual remote working looks attractive with the absence of the commute, more flexible use of time and a better work-life balance but there are a whole heap of issues you need to be aware of that can flip the scales in the other direction. For most people home-working represents a revolution in how they run their lives. Before committing to this you should decide if it's right for you and look at strategies that will allow you to enjoy the good stuff while embracing the minuses. We'll give you a whole lot of ideas on that.

There has never been a better time to be a remote worker. Make no mistake this way of working is growing exponentially, just try googling 'remote jobs' you'll see lots of jobs advertised in a very wide range of disciplines and this is only the tip of the iceberg. My e-mail inbox is regularly full of offers to improve my website and/or its standing in Google searches from individuals and companies all over the world. Look at sites like **freelancer.com** and **Fiverr** and you can see global talent marketing itself to provide services remotely. We'll give you some tips on how to find remote jobs and market yourself in this growing area of work.

2

CAN YOU HANDLE WORKING REMOTELY?

Introduction

Home and remote working is already growing fast and is set to see a step change expansion in the aftermath of the COVID-19 pandemic.

There has already been a very strong trend towards home-working in companies with large numbers of office based staff and many younger employees are seeing the freedom to work remotely as an essential rather than nice-to-have. In addition employees with children view remote working as a way of balancing the dual demands of parenting and career. Once people have worked remotely they are less happy to return to the daily grind of the commute.

Most employers, once they've got past the 'if I can't see them how do I know they're working' mind-set also see this as a positive development with the opportunity to make huge cost savings in office rent. A 2016 study conducted by Vodafone involving 8,000 global employees and employers[1] found that three-quarters of companies worldwide had already switched to more flexible working practices. 61% believe that it had increased the company's profits and 83% reported a boost in productivity.

75%
Of companies worldwide indicated they had introduced flexible working policies

83%
Indicated a boost in productivity

61%
Stated they had increased profits as a result

Source Vodafone 'Flexible: friend or foe?' 2016

In 2016, Dell announced plans to further expand its telecommuting and remote work initiatives, citing $12 million in annual savings from reduced office space cost[2].

Companies who need to source scarce skills that they can't find locally are now finding that they can easily tap into a much larger pool of highly skilled resource world-wide. The world's most valuable resource is knowledge and the market for services and skills is becoming truly global. In a crowded world, limiting migration is being seen as a political priority for a growing number of governments and in this environment the trend towards employing remote off-shore expertise is only likely to grow.

However while there are many positives, some people find it hard to adapt to home and remote working. Being unable to physically meet people can lead to frustration and insecurities and give rise to fears that the social element of work will be gone or considerably diminished. Feelings of isolation and stress are not uncommon in remote workers. So it's important to go into remote working with open eyes, acknowledge the potential issues and deploy strategies to lessen any negative impacts.

"Since you all requested to 'work remotely',
I guess you're happy with this relocation."

The pluses and minuses of remote work

While remote working has lots of positives it can also give rise to feelings of loneliness, isolation and stress.

The positives of working remotely

There are a number of pitfalls that you need to be aware of before embarking on a journey into home-working, but without doubt there are some real advantages for individuals.

Flexibility is an important one, particularly for parents who can find it a lot easier to balance career with child care and spend more time with their kids. There was something special about being able to pick my kids up from school when they were young, but sadly having to commute for an hour each way into work meant I was rarely able to do this. So working from home may well provide you with the chance to build a better relationship with your family and potentially reduce child care costs. Even without children, the opportunity to follow a less regimented life than one that consists of commute, work and commute again appeals to a lot of people.

Flexibility isn't just about family it's also about structuring your day the way you want to. If you want to take the morning off and work late then there's no funny looks to contend when you roll into the office in the afternoon. Maybe you want to have a quick nap after lunch (just try that in the office!) or watch a film in the morning. It's all possible when you're working from home.

A lot of people thrive in an environment where there's less scrutiny. Less pressure and freedom from feeling that the boss is breathing down your collar ironically boosts productivity with many employees.

Waving goodbye to commuting is usually quoted as the major attraction for remote workers and most of us can easily appreciate the allure of this. Commuting either by car or public transport can be unpleasant and frustrating, not to mention expensive. Worse still during the COVID-19 epidemic commuting actually became dangerous!

There is a certain irony that the types of roles most likely to be conducive to remote working are predominantly based in cities e.g. Finance, Marketing and IT, as are the people who fill those roles. Accommodation in big cities is usually pricey and so tight for space that it doesn't rate as the ideal home-working environment.

However those employees or contractors who know they can reliably work from home should be able to locate themselves in lower cost, more spacious and almost certainly more pleasant accommodation out of town. Working remotely has the potential to give you the best of both worlds, access to the big city and all of the opportunities that brings for both work and entertainment while living a better lifestyle in a less crowded and less polluted environment outside of town. I know a computer programmer who works remotely and lives five minutes from a beach with his young family. His prime motivation is to bring his children up in a pleasant environment close to good schools. The only real limitation on where he can live is the quality of the internet connection.

Many people find they can be far more productive in a remote environment. The lack of the type of distractions encountered in an office helps concentration and there is potential to structure your day to maximize productivity. I worked with a client on the East Coast of the States. Because of the time difference this allowed me to reserve my mornings for uninterrupted desk work and the afternoons for meetings, but with a little discipline you can achieve this sort of split wherever your customers are.

You'll almost certainly be richer too. Commuting costs money, so does that wardrobe of smart work clothes and the packaged sandwiches and barista coffee you just can't resist. Having said that you may need to work hard on your willpower with the fridge and cookie tin only a few paces away!

Isolation, loneliness and stress

This may sound a bit alarmist but these are factors you need to consider if you're working from home.

The lack of the sort of support organisation you'd expect to have around you in an office based set up can quickly lead to feelings of isolation. Hopefully you'll be working for an enlightened company who have thought out how to get remote workers up to speed and provide a good induction programme but the chances are this won't be the case. Not knowing what you have to do, who you need to ask and where to find information can be both frustrating and stressful. It's also very easy for management to fall into an 'out of sight out of mind' mentality with remote workers and this can lead to feelings of being left out and lack of trust.

"I've been feeling a lot of work related stress."

From my experience of working remotely, I've found it's easy to slip into feelings of uncertainty about what value you're adding. I've found myself thinking that doing my job well wasn't enough and feeling pressure to be seen to be always making an impact. My way of compensating for that was to work harder, to try to do a better job than I ever would have face-to-face. In most work situations our performance is rated against our peers. One of the issues with remote work is that often there is no clear benchmark, making it much harder to measure your effectiveness against others doing similar jobs. These and similar behaviors are easy to fall into as a remote worker and can result in overwork, anxiety and stress. A 2017 report from Eurofound on remote working[14] indicated that 41% of remote workers experienced high stress levels as opposed to 25% of office based employees.

Boundaries between work and leisure have a tendency to blur. With the commute gone and the work computer in the next room there's a strong temptation to keep working or to squeeze a couple of hours of work in before bedtime or at the weekend, particularly if you're up against a deadline. This is exacerbated further if you're working on an international project when you may be called into meetings late at night for you but midday for everyone else. One of the projects I worked on involved a meeting that included European, Middle and Far Eastern and an Australian attendee. The Australian attendee always used to joke that he was attending in his pyjamas, because of the time differences. All of this can take a toll on sleep patterns and mental health.

Loneliness is also an acknowledged issue for home workers and tends to be exacerbated by long and potentially anti-social hours. The Epson Ecotank Survey of 1000 freelancers[10] found that while there were plenty of positives expressed for working from home, 48% of those interviewed said they had experienced loneliness and 46% said that it was isolating. In addition 29% said they missed being part of a team and 32% missed the social aspects of being in an office. For many people, particularly those in repetitive jobs, a large part of their job satisfaction comes from meeting people and social interaction.

It's important before you commit to an extended spell of remote working that you appreciate these dangers. There are some simple and sensible things you can do to lessen their impact and help you enjoy working remotely:-

- Be kind to yourself, acknowledge that remote working can be stressful and don't beat yourself up if things go wrong

- Work on your social life. Make sure your social life outside of work is as good as you can make it. Get out of the house, meet people, do things, have fun!

- Take part in remote social activities with your team (see Chapter 3 – How to Build Successful Remote Teams)

- Stay fit. Fitness is important and if you pick the right sport, also a social outlet. I play a lot of tennis and try to make sure I fit my work schedule around my tennis life when I'm working remotely. Exercise relaxes you and boosts endorphins and is a real antidote to being stuck at home all day working. A long walk, a run or a bike ride is good.

- Look after your body. Maybe fitness is a step too far if you're not an active sort of person, but be aware what hours slumped over a laptop can do to your body. This applies to office work too, but in the quieter, more absorbed atmosphere of remote work, it's a lot easier to just obsessively plough on. Staying seated at a desk for hours on end can give you back and neck ache and generally screw your body up. Getting up and walking around frequently is good advice. A study from Columbia University[17] recommended getting up from your desk every 30 minutes. They found that switching out 30 minutes of sedentary time over the course of the day for 30 minutes of low-intensity activity reduced the risk of an early death by about 17%. You might also want to look at Yoga or Pilates as a way of stretching the wrinkles out of your body. What you put into your body also counts, drink plenty of water and if working at home makes you snack more then buy in some healthy snacks rather than loading up on fat, sugar and salt.

- Look after your mind. Bill Gates and Paul McCartney are two amongst many who meditate every morning and swear by its benefits. Twenty minutes meditation before throwing yourself into your day's work starts you off feeling calm and clear minded and provides a break between home life and work life. It's too easy when you're working remotely to wake up with your head full of thoughts about work, rush through breakfast and just get stuck into it. Think of it as replacing your highly stressful commute with some moments of calm and inner peace. I'd highly recommend Quiet The Mind by Matthew Johnstone as a short and amusing way of learning how to meditate[20].

- Be aware of 'Zoom Fatigue'[19]. From research carried out by Gianpiero Petriglieri, and Marissa Shuffler you're more likely to experience fatigue on videoconferences because the brain has to work a lot harder. Petriglieri observes that not only is it much harder to relax into conversation naturally but we're also constantly trying to try to find the non-verbal content that we usually just absorb without having to think about it. Our minds are together but our bodies are not. Shuffler points out that seeing yourself and also seeing everyone apparently staring at you when you talk can also make you feel like you're constantly performing and that can be exhausting too. Their remedy is to avoid loading yourself with back-to-back video meetings and try turning the camera off if you feel too observed.

- Make use of the flexibility. Working from home gives you flexibility, so take advantage of this. Give yourself a lunch-break, go for a walk, watch some TV or maybe part of a film each day or enroll in a daytime class where you can switch off and meet people. Make sure you're not tied to a desk all day every day for hours on end. It's not good for your physical or mental well-being.

- Make a daily schedule. While the flexibility you get is great it's also good to have a structure to your day and to your week. Take time at the start of the day and start of the week to organise how you're going to utilise your time.

- Follow a plan and/or to do list. I've found myself at the end of days, weeks or even months trying to work out just what I've achieved. Clearly this can be the case for office work too, but you seem to feel it more when you're working remotely. Set yourself targets and give yourself a mini pat on the back when you achieve them.

- Be organised. If you're going to prove your professional credibility you need to be organised. Make sure you have the facts at your fingertips. Do your homework and understand what is going on. If there are gaps in your knowledge then try hard to fill them. If you're working in an unfamiliar technical area, carry out your own research to get up to speed.

- You might want to consider working in a shared physical space to increase your opportunities for social interaction. This could be a coffee shop with Wi-Fi (as long as security isn't compromised) or one of the many co-working spaces that are springing up aimed mainly at one person businesses. Check out a **Jelly** – you'll find them online and on **Eventbrite**. The concept is to get remote workers together to work and collaborate (but not feel pressured to sell) in a shared place at no cost to the user.

- Know when to stop work. One of the biggest issues with home workers is that they don't know when to stop and can end up working long days and weekends, risking stress and burnout.

- Reduce the unnecessary distractions. Distraction and lack of concentration can be an issue for remote workers. This isn't just about getting today's work done, it can also place a strain on you and make you doubt your ability to finish things. Put some rules in place e.g. no news, sports and social media sites until your lunch break or the end of your working day. Use the 'Do Not Disturb' setting on your smartphone with exceptions so you can still receive calls but delay the noise from social media and messaging until you're ready to accept it.

- Try to adapt to different time zones. If you're working on an international project think about how you're going to organise your day. If you're working with people on say the west coast of America then think about matching their hours or at least extend the overlap between your hours and theirs.

- Get enough sleep. Just because the office is so close to your bed it doesn't make it a good idea to go straight from the one to the other! Give yourself a decent gap between work and going to bed. The overstimulation associated both with work and staring at screens close to bed time is likely to result in disturbed sleep. You may also want to take advantage of the flexibility of remote work by taking a nap during the day – it's amazing how much this can recharge your batteries, but make sure you set an alarm if you do. "Sorry I missed your important meeting because I fell asleep" really isn't a good line.

Your home office

If you're going to make remote working work for you then you need to have a decent home office. It may initially seem ok to work from the kitchen table but for a whole host of reasons that's likely to become difficult to sustain. Working with any set-up where the screen isn't at eye level is highly likely to result in neck, shoulder and back pain and if continued can cause permanent damage to your health.

There will be times where you'll need privacy or to demonstrate it to the other people on the call. Other members of your family wandering in and out of shot won't exactly help.

The best environment is one where you can cut yourself off mentally and physically from your home life. As well as providing privacy, this also achieves a level of separation that helps discourage you from merging home and work life. If you don't have this then you should think hard about whether you can make remote working work for you long term.

Once you have your home office you need to be able to set yourself up to facilitate working from home. A decent wide desk so you can have everything you need in front of you, an ergonomic chair with plenty of adjustment to give you proper back and neck support.

Ideally you want a wireless mouse and keyboard and a monitor that you can have at head level – the top third of the screen should be at eye level, the keyboard and mouse at elbow height with your back straight, not hunched over the screen.

You'll probably be spending a good proportion of your working life videoconferencing. Wearing a headset for hours on end can be very tiring and starts to heat your head up. There are lightweight headsets which are better but the set up I prefer is a high quality webcam with a good microphone and the sort of lightweight headphones you'd use for listening to music. There are plenty of good webcams out there and lots of video reviews on YouTube but I'd personally recommend a midrange **Logitech** or **Microsoft webcam**. You generally get what you pay for and the cheaper webcams either have poor microphones or poor cameras or both!

Try to make your home office as pleasant and light an environment as possible within the constraints of what's you can do in your home. If you're going to spend all or most of your working life in your home office then you'd better like being there!

Self-esteem and morale

I'll talk a lot about body language and the frustrations and difficulties that arise because of the lack of it in the next chapter, but there are other aspects of remote working that can start to gnaw away at your feelings of self-esteem.

Meetings can be a very different experience. Often one or a few people can dominate a meeting and it can be very hard to break in and get across what you need to. At the other end of the scale, it's also easy to find someone talking over you. Videoconferencing doesn't lend itself well to working out when you can break in or to warding people off who are trying to talk over you. It's much easier to sense the time to either interrupt or to not break in from people's body language in face-to-face meetings. Sometimes video calls can dissolve into a cacophony of noise as several people try to break in at the same time while someone is already speaking. This can be both frustrating and morale draining, but it's important to see this as limitations of the technology and the general situation and not let it get you down.

When you do speak at meetings it can feel a bit scary, given you're always addressing the entire meeting. This tends to be further exacerbated by a screen full of faces staring at you, none of whom seems to be reacting to what you're saying. This can be unnerving and sag your morale and some people find it difficult. One way of addressing this is that many videoconferencing packages allow you to split a meeting into smaller break-out groups and then come back together towards the end of the meeting. Often this can be better than all sitting together with some people listening and not contributing for a good part of the meeting. Suggest this to the person who called the meeting if you think this would work better for you.

Think about how you want to appear to the other participants in the videoconference. You see yourself on the screen in videoconferences and it's very easy to start thinking what an unkempt wreck you look and how the camera seems to be exaggerating all of your wrinkles and making you look older than you are. Just because you can roll out of bed straight into your office there's no reason to look like that just happened. You may want to dress smartly and fix your hair and face, plus very importantly sort out the lighting in your office. Most people look pretty ghastly when lit from the side. Face-on lighting makes you look a whole lot better and has a tendency to mask your imperfections (assuming you have any!). Also aim to have the camera at eye level. Below doesn't really work unless you like the Bohemian Rhapsody effect and above doesn't tend to present the best image of you either. If the camera is on top of the screen and hard to move, this may mean you moving instead by changing your chair adjustment during videoconferences. This may all sound a bit facile but don't underestimate it. If you look good then you feel good and when you're working remotely, it's important to keep your moral high.

> **Key remote working recommendations**
> - *Working remotely has lots of positives*
>   - *Freedom from commuting*
>   - *Better balance of work and family life*
>   - *More flexibility in your life*
>   - *Live somewhere nicer – all you need is a decent internet connection*
>   - *Save money on commuting, work, clothes and cappuccinos!*
> - *But you must guard against the negatives*
>   - *Feelings of isolation, loneliness and stress*
>   - *Lack of the office support organisation*
>   - *Feeling pressure to make an impact*
>   - *Boundaries between work and leisure can blur*
> - *Stay fit, work on your social life, look after yourself, follow a plan, structure your days, check out a **Jelly**, know when to stop, reduce distractions, get enough sleep*
> - *Set up a home office if you can*

Finding remote work

Working remotely has become far more mainstream in the last few years. As long as you have saleable skills, it isn't difficult to earn a good living as a remote worker.

There are a variety of ways you can work remotely. The first for many people is with their existing employer who may offer the opportunity to work from home for some or all of the week. I ran a home-working trial for a large UK company over 15 years ago and despite the poorer technology available then, the trial was an unreserved success. However when I presented my findings to the board of directors I received a frosty reception. How do we know people are working if we can't see them? How do we know they're not sitting in front of the TV all day? How can managers get hold of employees when they need to? They rejected my proposal to expand the pilot. Things have moved a long way since then with far more sophisticated technology available to facilitate, monitor and manage remote working. Employers in the main don't feel the insecurity and potential loss of control that those board members did.

So if you're looking for a new role, while not many years ago this might have been seen as an odd question to ask at an interview, don't be afraid to ask a potential new employer what their policy is on working from home. You'll usually be met with a constructive response. Some big employers positively encourage employees to work from home. It keeps their overheads low and may also fit in with what they're trying to sell to their customers. In those early days for remote working when I was running that pilot we talked to both IBM and BT who were enthusiastically embracing it. This was the way they saw things going and were positioning themselves to learn lessons from their own experiences which would help them market solutions to their customers.

The other main routes into remote working are running your own business from home or to look directly for remote roles through the many websites and agencies advertising them.

There is little doubt that after the experience of the COVID-19 epidemic that remote working opportunities will rocket. As a very small example, I've been attending a French conversational class for a couple of years. It's run by a teacher who leads a number of classes on different days and in locations within a 20 mile radius. During the COVID-19 lockdown the group went online and used Zoom. This worked very well and suddenly, with its geographic limitations removed, started attracting members from much further afield. She also runs Spanish conversational classes and has attracted two British participants who live in Spain who want to improve their language skills. Suddenly almost by accident, the owner had transformed a local business into an internet one and all of the potential growth opportunities that might lead to.

Lots of small businesses are run remotely, some have an office with a small number of people but all of their clients are remote, some have no office but come together as a team to work effectively. I've been working as a consultant to a small American IT company for a few years. Most of their employees work from home and a number are contractors. This works very well for them. Their overheads are low and as business expands and contracts it's very easy to flex their workforce.

Remote jobs

So if you're wondering what jobs are available to be carried out remotely you can start with the thought that almost any office based job could be carried out remotely and carry on from there. Jobs recently advertised include:

- IT developers
- IT testers
- IT support
- Copy/Content editors
- Customer service
- Graphic design/Photo editing
- Sales consultant
- Marketing and communications manager
- Education/On-line learning
- Health
- Counselling
- Recruitment
- Clothes design
- Procurement
- Translator
- On-line journalism

- Data analyst

- Insurance claims

- Project manager

- Growth hacker

- Payments processing

- Mortgage broker

- Bid/Proposal writer

- Litigation attorney

And of course there are many more. The world of remote work is expanding and is truly international. There are some roles that will of course never be remote e.g. manufacturing, construction, hospitality and personal services such as hairdressing and dentistry, but there are thousands of remote jobs advertised weekly.

Remote job websites

So if you're looking for remote work you need to think more broadly than you would for office based work. Remote work is international and while there will be some restrictions where local knowledge is required, if you have a skill such as computer programming, project management, copy writing, marketing or procurement these are in demand worldwide.

All job sites ask you to enter the role you're looking for and a location. Most but not all will allow you to enter 'remote' as location. This works for **Linkedin, Monster, JobServe, Indeed, Glassdoor** and many others.

On top of this there are specialist remote work sites such as **Remote Jobs, Flexjobs, We Work Remotely and Workew** who only advertise remote jobs.

If you search for **#remotejobs** on **Twitter** you'll get lots of hits for remote work. You can also join **Facebook** groups set up for remote jobs, just search for **remote jobs** and you'll find lots of groups where jobs are advertised and where you can post saying you're looking for a remote job – you'd be surprised how effective that can be.

The jobs advertised will be both permanent and contract positions but if you do intend working for yourself or setting up your own business to market your skills then you're better to look at the gig economy – people offering temporary positions or complete pieces of work for a fixed fee.

Working for yourself

This is an ever growing and truly international market and there are some good people out there who will help you market your talents.

Toptal – short for Top Talent – they claim to have the top 3% of the world's talent to hire on a contract basis. Toptal work more like a traditional recruitment company but focus on supplying quality individuals. If you think you have a top talent then try Toptal.

Freelancer - is probably one of the longest established sites for contract work with a huge number of contractors registered for work on it (they claim 15 million) and a very wide range of skills. Buyers post work and contractors bid for the work.

Upwork and **Guru** – are more recent arrivals with a similar business model to Freelancer.

Fiverr – works in the opposite way to Freelancer, you post your services and rates and buyers find you and employ you, but be aware that Fiverr rates as the name suggest start very low. Fiverr has been accused of encouraging a race to the bottom as sellers from all over the world try to undercut each other on rates. If you use Fiverr you'll need a strategy to upsell more expensive services or you'll work very hard for little income!

Most of these sites deal with invoicing the customer and take a cut of what you earn.

Of course you can forget all of the above, build your own website and market yourself. In fact you could use **Fiverr** to find a website designer and get exactly what you want built very cheaply. As all small business owners will tell you, setting up a business is easy, it's getting customers that's difficult and the best way to do this is through contacts rather than advertising. I'd recommend you carefully cultivate contacts wherever you work. If it's in your mind to work for yourself at some point then connect through **LinkedIn** with everyone you meet, but also invite work acquaintances to become **Facebook** friends – you might want to have two Facebook accounts, one for personal friends and the other for work acquaintances, but it's a very effective way of staying in people's consciousness and contacting them if you're looking for work.

If you have to rely on advertising then try free posts on **Twitter**, **Facebook** and **LinkedIn** first and try to work out what captures most attention. If you're selling a scarce skill then try to use **SEO** to get on the **first page of a Google search**…this is of course easier said than done and can cost a lot of money to achieve.

Getting through a remote interview

To some extent a remote interview mirrors a face-to-face one but there are some important differences. Know your job history, why you want to move, research the company you're hoping to join, rehearse your answers to what are your strengths and weaknesses and where you see your career in 5 years' time as normal, but there are a few other tips for remote interviews.

Self-motivation and initiative are important qualities to get across. You're out there in the big world, not just five minutes' walk down the office, so the last thing a prospective employer wants is someone who needs to be spoon-fed every item of work.

In remote work everyone has to try a bit harder to communicate. You don't want to come across as someone who really wants to work remotely because you don't like people (Ok it might be true…just don't let anyone know!).

You'll need to convey that you can handle the lifestyle and attendant pressures we've described earlier. If you've done it before and can provide references to prove it then all the better.

You need to emphasise that you're comfortable using the sort of remote work tools that we describe in Chapter 4 - Technology – messaging, e-mail, videoconferencing and management tools.

All employers should be concerned that you have a suitable space to work in. The employer may have health and safety concerns as well as wanting to be assured that disruptions and noise are not going to degrade your productivity.

And there are some questions you should ask. Ask about their support for remote workers and if they have an established onboarding process. If you get as far as a job offer, you could ask if they have other remote workers who you could talk to before accepting the offer. Find out what tools they use, how you will be managed and how they encourage everyone to feel part of a team.

> **Recommendations on finding remote work**
> - *Permanent employees*
>   - *Ask your current employer if you can work remotely*
>   - *Don't be afraid to ask a potential employer if you can work at home*
>   - *Some big employers encourage home working*
> - *Where to find a remote job*
>   - *Check out traditional job sites and set your location to 'Remote'*
>   - *Check out specialist remote job sites*
>   - *Search Twitter for **#remotejobs***
>   - *Join Facebook remote jobs groups*
>   - *Work for yourself and market yourself on freelance remote work sites*
> - *To get through a remote interview emphasise*
>   - *You are self-motivated*
>   - *You're a good communicator*
>   - *You can handle the lifestyle and attendant pressures*
>   - *You're comfortable using remote working technology*

3
HOW TO BUILD SUCCESSFUL REMOTE TEAMS

Introduction

Team building isn't easy. Building a remote team is twice as difficult.

I've already talked about recruitment in the previous chapter and it's clearly important in a remote team to make sure you can find people who will fit in and who are self-motivated. But once you've assembled your diverse team possibly based in different countries with a variety of customs and cultures, then it's important to turn your group of talented individuals into a real team.

Doing this with an office based team isn't easy, doing it with a remote team is full of new and interesting challenges. I've broken this chapter into:

- Teamwork – how do you build a feeling of team

- Communication – is key to a successful team

- Respecting different cultures – don't alienate or upset half of your team because of insensitivity

- Country specifics – basic stuff that you may find varies in other legislations

If you can achieve the first three well, then you'll have a productive and happy team. None of this is easy. Remote working is hard for employees who will need feedback and encouragement from their managers and hard for managers who are often a lot better at managing staff when they can see them. Everyone has to work that little bit harder to make it happen.

Teamwork

Working as an effective team makes everyone happier and more productive. People often don't pay enough attention to teamwork in office based teams, it's absolutely vital for remote teams.

Think about how you organise

The COVID-19 crisis brought about a rapid forced acceleration in remote working. Better to have employees doing some work at home than no work at all in lockdown. Understandably work organisation was tweaked the minimum to get everyone working.

This is far from ideal and before diving into remote working you need to put some thought into how you are going to organise things. Does the current office organisation make sense in a remote set up? Do you have the tools you need to effectively manage and organise people remotely? How are you going to integrate remote and office based teams? How do you plan to assess staff performance and identify both the poor performers who you may want to coach or discipline and the star performers who you want retain and promote? How do you induct new employees into the company and into their roles? Are you happy for everyone to determine their own hours as long as they get the work done or do you need to mandate core hours that everyone has to cover? What is your policy on availability so you know you can contact employees? How are you going to regulate behaviour between employees?

These are all questions that you need to address. Once you've come up with the answers then it's a good idea to put a remote working 'contract' in place. A set of rules that employees have to sign up to so everyone is clear where they stand.

Pretty much all companies have processes but few have them documented. If you're going to adapt and improve your processes for remote work, now is the opportunity to document them. Think also about how you could use the tools we talk about in Chapter 4 – Technology to manage and regulate your processes. These tools will allow you to run projects and/or implement workflows to help integrate both office based and remote teams. Look at methodologies like **Lean** and **Six Sigma** to analyse, document and improve your processes. Both will help identify and eliminate wasted effort within processes, improve work flows, speed up work, increase quality and reduce errors.

Working remotely will reduce the usual level of communication and can make it hard for employees to establish facts. This can slow everyone down or in the worst case end up with customers being given answers and advice on a best guess basis. So look to establish Wikis and/or Knowledge Bases so that everyone is working off the same information and can find what they need instantly. See Chapter 4 – Technology for more detail on these products.

Many people seem to lose inhibitions when working over a video link, a bit like the polite person who transforms behind the wheel of a car. When they're on a videoconference they feel secure and a little detached in the warm safety of their home and become less inhibited in what they say than would be the case face-to-face. The same can apply to communication via e-mail and messaging. If you let this run out of control it can sour relations between employees and destroy team work. Make sure you make all employees at all levels aware of what is acceptable and that respect must be shown at all times.

Managers need to work a lot harder to make sure they stay in touch with and be available to their team. The type of interactions that happen naturally daily and hourly in an office disappear. Employees can feel uncared for and isolated and managers less in touch and not in control. Staff appraisals are also tied to this. People need and expect to be treated fairly and managers have to know who is and who isn't performing, who they can trust and who they need to keep tabs on. This isn't an easy transition to make, especially for managers. Weekly one-to-ones between a manager and each of their team members are a must. These will be time consuming but ultimately worthwhile for both employee and manager. You need to be able to identify exceptional work or effort above and beyond the norm and reward it as a minimum with a thank you. But better still, but you'd be amazed how much difference a bottle of wine or box of chocolates arriving on the doorstep with a nice thank you note makes.

The power of small talk

Most people need small talk (as well as professional work talk) to interact well. In fact many historians believe that human language evolved primarily as a way of communicating gossip[9]

So you might want to think about a 'Wall of Fame'. Include a photo of each team member and a short description of their background, interests and hobbies. It can live in a shared on-line space that everyone can get to. Once you have the 'Wall of Fame' it's then really easy to expand into more detail around interests and hobbies, with images and videos posted of employees playing tennis or football or if they're animal lovers, cute images of their dog, cat or maybe even pet rat.

The Wall facilitates small talk. It lets everyone on the team know what their colleagues look like and it provides scope for conversation – hey you're a movie buff, keen cyclist, music lover. It opens up everyone's background and interests and that helps build the feeling of being in a team. A little small talk goes a long way to growing a sense of being included and part of something that's often lacking in geographically dispersed teams.

One of the guys I worked for used to start their weekly meetings by asking each of the attendees to say (briefly!) what they had been up to over the weekend. It's tricky to do this for a big meeting but if you've a number less than seven it's worth a try – again it's about getting people to open up and know each other better.

People are notoriously bad at arriving on time for meetings. Use that waiting time to chat rather than just staring into mid-air or catching up on e-mails. Keep a cache of topics, check what's in the news, but don't get too carried away. Politics and the team's love lives are better left well alone.

Social Activities

It may sound a bit odd but you can run social activities remotely and they're a very effective way of building teamwork.

I know of a group who meet remotely after work to play games and have a couple of drinks while they're doing it – this isn't at all that uncommon, so ask for a volunteer social organiser and get going.

Here are some ideas:-

- A quiz night is always a good ice breaker and if your organisation is big enough then you can break into teams. A number of videoconferencing tools facilitate break-out groups making this easy to do. Buy a few drinks and it becomes a pub quiz! You can either research and set the questions yourself or use sites like **TriviaMaker** and **TriviaBliss** to produce the questions for you.

- Charades works well over a video link. Come up with an idea, say whether it's a book, film, TV show, play, person or something from another category and then act it out starting by saying how many syllables you're acting out.

- Movie night. Vote on what movie you all want to watch and share a Netflix, YouTube or Amazon Prime screen. There are a whole host of apps and browser add-ons specifically designed for this, try **TwoSeven**, **Netflix Party** and **Watch2Gether**. They'll allow you to synchronise watching videos with your friends together with a chat window so you can all make comments about the movie while it's running.

- Smartphone Apps. If you like word games you might want to give **WordswithFriends** or **Scrabble Go** a try. They're both Android and iOS word game apps. You can have a videoconference running at the same time as you're playing the game on your phones.

- Pictionary. If your videoconferencing package supports whiteboards then it's easy to play Pictionary but even if it doesn't pen and paper in front of the camera works just as well. You can use **Pictionary Random Word Generator** to come up with words.

- Two truths, one lie. Really great icebreaker. Each person on the video call tells two true things about themselves and one lie. Everyone else has to guess which is which.

- Murder Mystery Party. Why not set up a murder mystery party. Try **The Murder Mystery Store** or **My Mystery Party**, both sell virtual games relatively cheaply.

- **Donut** is an extension to Slack, a popular workplace messaging tool. It pairs people randomly together in your company for a 30 minute chat as a way of getting to know people. Messaging is less pressured but you might want to do this face-to-face on a videoconference instead.

- Plant growing competitions. This works a treat. The idea is that each participant (you might want to make it teams) buys a packet of seeds of exactly the same plant. Everyone then plants, tends and grows. Pick something like chillies, cucumbers or tomatoes that produce a crop, set an end date and compare who produced the biggest crop or most fruits or the healthiest plant. It's amazing how competitive people get. This is very involving and lasts a while too. Get a senior manager to judge it.

- Karaoke is great fun and a little less exhibitionist than banging it all out in a bar. Search YouTube for 'karaoke' and you'll find lots of karaoke videos complete with rolling lyrics displayed on the screen. Either share the YouTube screen in the videoconference or better still use one of the video sharing apps like **Watch2Gether** or **TwoSeven** to make sure you all synchronise and then you can watch your colleagues put heart and soul into their performances over the video link.

- Come dine with me. Pick a (preferably simple) recipe off an internet food site, order the ingredients in and then prepare and eat it together. Hard to do without a laptop given you need to be mobile, moving from kitchen to dinner table, but good fun if you can make it work and you can involve family members too!

- You might want to offer employees activities like Yoga, Tai Chi, Pilates or Zumba and fund an instructor. Activities like Zumba are good because they're fun, involving and everyone has the chance to make a fool of themselves! All will work over a remote link.

- Foreign language conversational groups work well over remote links too and can also help integrate teams where different languages are spoken.

- You can bring in guest speakers to talk on a range of interesting topics at lunchtimes.

- There are organisations who will organise remote social activities for you, for instance **petri** who will provide you with a schedule of fun, wellness and team building activities each month. They charge by subscription but take a lot of the hassle of running stuff out of your hands.

These are just examples of what you can do. You can find even more ideas online or why not set up a social committee and let them come up with creative ideas to get everyone more involved. You'll need to experiment to get the balance right, but I'd strongly recommend trying some of these.

Help everyone settle in

It's always hard when you join a new organisation. How do you do things here? What are the rules and policies? Who do I ask if I've got a question? How do I get IT support? It's doubly hard if you work remotely and it's very easy to get lost in the new organisation and start to despair. So if you're setting up an entire remote organisation or employing remote workers to expand an office based team, it's absolutely vital that you:

- Have an induction pack and some form of training even if it's a chat followed by a question and answer session.

- Have clear rules and policies held in a shared accessible location. These would ideally be held on a Wiki or Knowledge Base (see Chapter 4 - Technology) to make the information accessible and easily searchable

- Have an up to date organisational chart

- Make it clear who you ask for what e.g. pay and employment conditions, IT support

Ideally have a single touch point for new employees to get help and settle in and not someone who's so busy that questions take hours or days to be serviced.

Meet Ups

Lots of companies organise regular meet-ups to get their remote and office based employees physically together. These are often badged 'Hackathons', a term that was originally about computer programmers getting together to hack out code but now seems to have been adopted more generally for these sort of business get-togethers. Clearly covering travel and hotels costs can make this an expensive event but I'd recommend it and the chances are you'll make your money back by improving teamwork and generating ideas to help everyone work better.

This works best if you meet regularly rather than a one-off meet-up that no-one gets around to organising again. Two or three of these each year is at the level of frequent but not too frequent, but this will vary by industry and application. In creative industries where bouncing ideas back and forth between team members is important then you may want to have more frequent meet-ups and organise these by project. Make sure you have a clear idea of what you want to get out of each meet-up and that you have a solid schedule of activities and workshops organised. As with any business away-day events you should use these meet-ups to openly address issues and problems and ask the team to come up with solutions. Meet-ups should be at least two days but I know plenty of companies who make them longer than that. Ideally try to have them finish on a Friday so you can have one really big get together on the Friday evening. If they're organised and run well these sessions gain so much in teamwork, problem solving and social binding. If you find it too daunting to organise then there are people who specialise in organising these gatherings. Try **Gravitywell** or **Hackathon.com**.

If you can't arrange this sort of event then try to encourage remote workers to meet each other face-to-face at least once. It's surprising how much difference this makes, usually creating a bond that helps communication and builds understanding and empathy.

Show your face

I've been in far too many videoconferences where everyone shuts down the video and sticks to audio. This is fine where the line bandwidth is poor or you have a huge number of participants but try to avoid it otherwise.

Don't worry about what anyone else on the call is doing, go on to video whenever possible, a real face is just that, not a disembodied voice. Even if you can't pick up their body language, let everyone see some of yours. Hardly anyone looks good on a video link, especially wearing a headset and your reading glasses but put your vanity to one side, being seen makes you a lot more real and credible.

Buy as high quality a camera as you can afford, a clear high definition image is better than a fuzzy one. Better cameras will also cope better with low or imperfect lighting. You may have to bear the sight of your wrinkles, grey hairs or blemishes in a little more focus than you'd like, but don't worry about it. It's all about projecting you as a person.

Also try to work in good lighting, so you don't look like some shady ghost that no-one can properly make out. As mentioned earlier face-on lighting tends to give the best results.

One other tip if you're working from home is to minimise the distractions behind your face. You want your audience concentrating on you, not your kids playing behind you or your underwear on the clothes dryer at the back of your room. Ideally have a part of your house set up as an office. Test how the backdrop looks and have it look clean and professional. Some videoconferencing packages allow you to blur your background or substitute an image. I'm not a big fan of either but this might be something you prefer.

Team meetings

In most remote work situations meetings are your lifeblood. They're where you talk with your team and really understand what's going on.

"A good team leader inspires intense loyalty."

In an office environment people pop around to your desk for a chat as a way of resolving issues and keeping you informed. Communication is more fluid and you're less likely to miss something. In a remote situation the opposite is true. To counter this I'd strongly recommend short daily meetings of no more than half an hour duration where everyone can air issues and discuss progress. Daily 'stand-ups' are one of the basic principles of the Agile IT development methodology where everyone in the meeting quite literally stands up. The meetings are meant to be short, so the idea behind everyone standing up is to make sure they don't get too comfortable. I've seen meeting rooms with no seats, just leaning bars, designed with this in mind. Of course when you're working in a remote team standing up isn't a great idea or the camera will probably may be trained on your midriff! However, the principle of frequent short meetings is good. Agile employs a simple agenda for its stand-ups, what did you do yesterday, what are you planning to do today and what impediments are you encountering. This won't work in every remote scenario, but it's not a bad starting point. It's also a good idea to keep an action list at these meetings to check no-one has forgotten what they'd previously committed to do.

You also need to think about disseminating information and keeping everyone apprised of what's going on, so I'd recommend a fortnightly slideshow where you do just that. Whether you're working remotely or not, don't underestimate the power of this. Everyone welcomes being kept informed about the bigger picture and it will also make it easier for them to put things into context when difficult decisions need to be made.

Review how it's going

Given the added uncertainties in working remotely, I'd strongly recommend that teams get together regularly to review how things are going. This can nip potential issues in the bud and even point to things that the team have fallen into a habit of doing that no-one has had the courage to suggest you stop.

It's good practice in any business to review what's working and what's not. It's important in these reviews to encourage everyone to be open and not be defensive. Make sure everyone knows they're there to identify what's going well and what's going badly so that they can improve the way that things are working. These meetings need to be managed carefully to avoid bruised egos and clashes of opinion, but if done well they can be both instructive and enjoyable.

Key Teamwork recommendations

- *Are you organised for remote work?*
  - *Don't just move the existing set-up into people's homes*
  - *Do you have the right tools to support remote work?*
  - *How are you going to integrate remote and office based teams?*
  - *What are your policies and limitations for remote workers?*
  - *How do you induct new remote employees?*
  - *How are you going to regulate behaviour between employees?*
- *Encourage small talk – try a Wall of Fame*
- *Organise remote social activities*
- *Put thought into how you help everyone settle in*
  - *Induction pack, organisation chart, who to ask*
  - *Key information on a knowledge base*
- *Hold regular physical meet-ups or Hackathons*
- *Show your face*
- *Hold daily team meetings*
- *Review how it's going*

Communication

People are built from head to toe for communication. It has been estimated that sixty five percent of communication is non-verbal much of which is lost in remote communication.

Let's face it, working remotely is mainly about communication. If you can't get that right, you won't get anything right. Teams of any sort regardless of their location work a whole lot better if they know what's expected of them, understand what the whole team is trying to achieve and are kept up to date on progress. This is a challenge for an office based team but a much bigger test for a remote team.

In this section I'm not going to talk about communications technology. There's plenty about that later in the book, but I am going to talk about how you communicate and what you need to consider in that.

So why would I need to do anything different just because I'm working remotely?

So you may be asking, what's so different about communication in remote teams? You might feel you're a pretty good communicator and just because you're in front of a camera with a headset on why would that be about to change? That's exactly what I thought when I worked on my first remote project. By the end I'd totally changed my view.

Working with a geographically distributed team is full of challenges that don't present themselves in local teams. These vary from poor technology, lack of non-verbal feedback, inability to have a quick chat to resolve things, to cultural differences, language and accent.

If you're going to make remote teams work then you need to fully understand the issues that working remotely brings. It's really easy to ignore these and just carry on as if people were sitting next to each other, but these things really matter when you're aiming to build a productive team. Teams who have members who work some of the week in the office and the remainder at home may feel they can be more relaxed about this but with this sort of arrangement it's common to not meet people on your team for many weeks. So getting communication right in this environment is just as important as it is with a fully remote team.

Coping with the loss of the non-verbal parts of communication

Communication consists of far more than the words that come out of your mouth. When you speak you move your hands, body, eyes and head continuously. All of these movements are closely coordinated with your speech and form the total communication[3].

Body language has been around for as long as Homo Sapiens and spoken words for between 50 and 100 thousand years, so we've had plenty of practice at both working in harmony. After Alexander Graham Bell patented the first telephone in 1876 we've barely had 150 years to adapt to using words without body language, so it's hardly surprising that we're not very good at it.

Ray L Birdwhistell an American anthropologist estimated from his research that 65 percent of communication is done non-verbally and more astonishingly that we can make and recognise around 250,000 facial expressions. Barbara and Allan Pease in The Definitive Book of Body Language[18] further estimated that body language is responsible for between 60 and 80 percent of the impact made in negotiations and that people form 60 to 80 percent of their first impression about a new person in less than four minutes.

Research by psychologists at Harvard University also showed how women are far better readers of body language than men. The researchers showed short films of a man and woman communicating with the soundtracks removed and asked the subjects to work out what they were talking about. The women read the situation correctly 87 percent of the time, while the men scored only 42 percent.

All of these non-verbal clues are lost in a voice-only meeting and many are lost or are considerably depreciated in a videoconference. This represents a huge loss in the richness and effectiveness of communication. As a result the potential for misunderstandings or misinterpretations is huge.

You need to be fully aware of the impact of separating the verbal and non-verbal parts of your communication. They won't be obvious to you of course, you'll still be pulling the usual expressions and doing the subtle stuff your face and body does when you communicate face-to-face but no-one else will be seeing it.

Non-verbal communication can consist of:

- Facial expressions

- Gaze and eye contact

- Eye expression - pupil dilation, blink rate, direction of gaze, degree of opening of the eyes and facial expression specifically in the eye area

- Gestures

- Posture

- Touch and smell

- Appearance

All of these convey a huge amount of information in addition to speech.

Facial expressions transmit emotion and social signals. This has been an area of detailed research by a number of eminent psychologists over the last fifty or more years. Argyle and Ingram in 1972 showed that when we communicate we look at each other frequently. We tend to make eye contact more when we're listening than talking (Exline and Winters 1965) and other studies have shown we make more eye contact with people we like and that eye contact is related to power. High power individuals maintain high levels of eye contact while both talking and listening (Ellyson, Dovido and Fehr 1981). There is of course no eye contact in an audioconference and our natural eye contact routine becomes very distorted in a videoconference.

Important information like approval and disapproval, happiness and anger or even surprise can be misjudged or lost without these non-verbal clues.

You must have found that you can get on with some people instantly whereas others seem much harder. This is often more because of the subtle workings of body language than what is actually being spoken. One study by Argle, Salter, Nicholson, Williams and Burgess in 1970 showed that non-verbal communication had five times as much influence on inter-personal relationships than did verbal.

Gestures of course can also transmit a lot of information and this varies from country to country. For instance Italians have a tradition of making use of hand and arm movements[4] in expressing themselves whereas the English tend to be more reserved. Voice itself can lead to assumptions about culture, social class, competence and personality type.

As a result you are likely to find it more difficult to work out how you're being viewed by people you interact with remotely, particularly over audio-only links. I've certainly found this.

Knowing when to speak on an audio-only call is also more difficult. When someone is speaking their body language gives off clues that say they don't want to be interrupted. The person interrupting also tends to provide a thank you or sorry in their body language when they interrupt. I worked on a project where I attended regular meetings remotely led by a senior manager who had a habit of pausing in thought mid-sentence before continuing to talk. The people in the room were getting body language signals that he was going to continue. I was on an audio-only link and found it very difficult to know when to break in. People also use body language to show they'd like to interrupt. Arms waving, body leaning forwards or head nodding as well as facial and eye expression can all indicate that you want to break into the conversation.

Research by Rutter and Stephenson in 1977 indicated the impact of this lack of non-verbal clues. It showed that there are fewer interruptions in audio conferences than when people meet face-to-face. Adding to this is that conversation on a video call isn't truly duplex. When one person talks everyone else has to shut up and wait their turn which makes communication very stilted. Because of the way the internet works where everything transmitted is first split up into packets, there is an almost unavoidable delay in video calls as everything is chopped up and then reassembled in real time also making interruption a little more fraught.

Non-verbal communication is also highly connected to culture with some gestures having often wildly varying meanings in different cultures. For example while good eye contact is praised and usual in the US and Europe, it can be seen as a sign of disrespect and challenge in other cultures, including Asian and African [11].

In some situations the lack of body language can work to your advantage. For instance, if you feel you have a very good case, it may be better to negotiate in audio-only because research shows that the person with the best case tends to win in audio-only negotiations. Face-to-face people have more of a tendency to be influenced by wanting the non-verbal feedback of approval and this can influence who wins the argument[5].

With this impaired sense of communication you can find yourself wondering 'did I just say something I shouldn't have?', 'did she really understand what I meant?' , 'Am I making an impact?'. I've also found in this arms-length environment that working out that people are becoming unhappy with you is a lot more difficult than you might think and clearly this can lead to very dangerous situations. Insecurities and misunderstandings can result, so you have to be a lot clearer and more careful when you express yourself and sometimes ask questions that you might have thought superfluous face-to-face. It's a good idea to confirm agreement or understanding of the key points discussed, at the end of a meeting.

As alluded to earlier, perhaps the worst situation is being a remote attendee at an office based meeting. You can't pick up the body language but all of the other attendees can, putting you at a definite disadvantage.

So be aware of what you are losing from the lack or impairment of non-verbal communication in both audio and videoconferences. There are strategies you can use to try to compensate but you'll never fully make up for what you lose.

Communication styles

There are a variety of communication styles. Everyone's style is a little different and this again is an area that psychologists have taken a keen interest in with vast swathes of literature written about it. We're not going to cover well-trodden ground but do want to emphasise that being an entirely remote presence tends to exaggerate your existing style, particularly where voice-only is available and no live video. You need to be aware of this and may want to reflect on your communication style. You will find with some thought and effort you can use words, phrasing and tone to counter this and so communicate more effectively.

Think about how you're getting information over. Be clear and ask questions if you have any suspicion that you've been misunderstood. Avoid aggression no matter how wound up you might feel. Keep it calm and polite and have a good scream in private once the meeting is over. Politeness not only keeps people happy but it's also more likely to achieve the desired results. Aggression is never a good idea but if you're working remotely then I'd go as far as saying it's a disaster. It's that much easier to turn people off and that much harder to repair the relationship after an outburst.

Without going over the top, try to behave in a way that is rewarding to the people you're interfacing with and try to take care of their self-esteem by praising effort and success.

Working remotely means in many cases you can't meet all of the people you're regularly interfacing with, but if it's feasible to meet any of them then I'd strongly recommend you do this and as early as possible. It adds a personal closeness that is hard to generate in any other way. We just seem to be able to communicate and get on better with people if we've had at least one face-to-face meeting with them. It seems to leave an imprint of intimacy that never goes away.

Active Listening

Being able to listen and absorb what you hear is an important skill in both our business and personal lives. Everyone seems to like a good listener and to complain about the person who likes the sound of their own voice. When you're working remotely, listening skills become especially important given the lack of non-verbal communication.

Research suggests that we only absorb between 25 and 50 percent of what we hear and given the greater opportunity for distraction, being remote is likely to reduce that further. To counter this, you might want to try to practice 'Active Listening'. Active Listening is used widely in the counselling community. It involves making a conscious effort to not only hear the words being communicated but the complete message.

This means paying careful attention to what is being communicated and not becoming distracted or bored. It's so easy to become distracted when you're in front of a computer on a conference call. There are e-mails and messages popping up in front of you, that report you have to finish by the end of the day and even a sports result to follow! There's nothing more embarrassing than becoming diverted in the middle of a call, only to be asked what you think about something that's being discussed and nothing more irritating than hearing the clicking of a mouse and keyboard coming from someone else on the call.

While someone is talking try to let them know that you're listening, avoid any distracting thoughts, ask them to clarify anything you're not sure about and summarise what they've said from time to time. Try not to come to judgements too quickly and to not interrupt them with counter arguments until you've absorbed what they're trying to convey.

Clearly if you were counselling someone, becoming bored or

distracted would be unforgivable and there's no way you would gain the confidence of your client. The same very much applies to remote work. You need to listen, understand and remember what is being said.

Nonviolent Communication (NVC)

Unresolved conflict destroys teams – conflict in a distributed team can be particularly toxic. Rivalries, vendettas and disagreements can fester much more readily in a remote environment, so it's important to do everything that you can to try to avoid this. Nonviolent communication is a way of addressing this by removing the negative and adversarial elements from conversation.

"Ready for your first lesson in conflict resolution?"

It's very easy to fall into negative feelings about the people you're interfacing with and to find yourself in adversarial situations. These aren't always easy to resolve face-to-face but have the potential to be far more corrosive when you're remote. The way you are viewed by people you've never met in person will largely be judged from what you say and how you express yourself. Being viewed as argumentative and judgemental isn't good. Being viewed as listening, calm and empathetic is likely to be regarded a lot more positively.

NVC has been used as a very effective resource for mediation in resolving conflicts and has been utilised in Rwanda, Sierra Leone, Bosnia and Croatia. Your workplace is unlikely to experience quite that level of conflict but NVC has proved to be very effective where people are trying to resolve disputes and disagreements.

Often our judgements get in the way of understanding what is happening. NVC teaches us to observe without evaluating, for example saying 'You're so obstructive' makes an evaluation of behaviour but doesn't actually tell us why you've made that evaluation. Replacing this with 'I've noticed that you disagree with a lot of my proposals' is better given it's factual and non-judgemental.

NVC was created by Marshall B Rosenberg [6] who explains that NVC is a process for more successful and empathetic communication and that there are four components to this process:

1. Observations
2. Feelings
3. Needs
4. Requests

Observation, as we've noted above is keeping judgement and criticism out of it and trying to discern and then communicate the facts.

It's natural to react to a critical, adversarial or accusatory statement with a defensive statement or counter attack. We tend to take these attacking statements personally and once the conversation starts moving down this track it has a habit of escalating to an unhappy conclusion. Rosenberg describes this as 'life-alienating conversation'. Other examples of life-alienating conversation are denial of responsibility, comparisons with others and the assertion that some people are simply 'bad' or evil'.

So having observed in a non-judgemental manner, the next step is to express your feelings. Identifying your emotions and being brave enough to express them helps you connect more effectively with others. So in our example after pointing out that they disagree with lots of your proposals, you might say 'and that makes me feel annoyed and frustrated'. NVC also instructs that you should take responsibility for your feelings, in other words explain why you feel that way. So we might say 'and that makes me feel annoyed and frustrated because it slows everything down and I'm feeling anxious that I won't be able deliver on time'. There is more than a subtle difference in this. The first statement solely blames the other party for making me annoyed and frustrated, the second recognises my thinking behind the feelings of annoyance and frustration and in particular states my needs (to deliver on time). Needs are the acknowledgement of the stimulus for our feelings.

So now we've managed to address what we've observed, how we're feeling and what our needs are without criticising, accusing, aggression or blaming. The next stage is to express what we would like to happen to make things good for us all - our 'request'.

This is a specific request for action that will fulfil our needs. It's important that this is a positive request, not a negative one. So 'stop disagreeing or the project won't deliver in time' won't do. Our request needs to be genuinely a request and not a demand and should not imply blame. It might be a series of requests and it must be specific, not vague or ambiguous or it may be impossible or very difficult to fulfil. So in our example, you could say 'would it be possible to schedule a short weekly meeting for us both to discuss my proposals at an early stage to get us both on the same sheet?'

So in summary, when someone communicates negatively, we can blame ourselves, blame others or alternatively sense the feelings and needs hidden in the other person's negative message. If we respond negatively we're unlikely to make much progress. The more we can express our feelings and needs the easier it is for the others to respond positively and with empathy.

So you may be thinking this all sounds a bit touchy feely and if you do think that, you'd be right. It's also quite difficult to do and if you're serious about trying this you should probably invest some time and money in training. However this is a widely used technique that has been proven to deliver excellent results in a wide variety of situations.

In a remote scenario being able to avoid conflict, listen and generate empathy is far more likely to produce results than some misguided confrontational approach. So if you're working remotely I'd strongly recommend that you familiarise yourself with NVC.

For more information on NVC please read Marshall B. Rosenberg's excellent book Nonviolent Communication - A Language for Life.

Open or closed questions

Open questions are ones that ask the respondent to think and reflect. They are unlikely ever to result in a one word answer. Closed questions are ones that can be answered with a single word or phrase often just yes or no. An example of a closed question would be 'You have finished it, haven't you' whereas an open question might go 'Can you give me a bit more detail on how the task is going?'

In some instances you do need a simple yes or no answer and closed questions are appropriate. However in a scenario where you're trying to encourage teamwork, it's better to let people speak rather than cutting them off with closed questions.

Humour

I like to build a bit of humour into the way I work. I often find the best way to diffuse a tricky situation is with a little humour, and well if you can't enjoy your work then life gets pretty dull. However while this is very effective face-to-face, from my experience I'm not convinced that this is the best approach when you're working remotely. A flippant comment in one culture (or even the same culture) may at best fall flat and at worst offend someone and if you're unable to see their reaction and them to see your smiling face then I think you're playing with fire. So by all means stay light but at all times business-like unless you feel you know the person you're talking to really well.

Written communication

Written communication comes in various forms, including e-mails, instant messages, reports and documents. Often there are tons of the stuff.

The main thing with all written communication is to bear in mind the people you're writing to. Your first language may not be theirs so keep the wording simple and straightforward.

For a large dispersed team, you might want to consider producing a newsletter especially if you can encourage all parts of the team to contribute. I ran an 18 month IT project with teams in India, US, Australia and England, meaning we had a large team spread across four continents. Making all of those guys feel like a single team was always going to be a challenge and one thing we did was to publish a newsletter. Hard work to bring it all together but it was well received and hopefully made a difference.

> **Key communication recommendations**
> - *Don't assume communicating with a remote team works the same as with a local one*
> - *Lack of non-verbal feedback, cultural, language, accent and technology issues will make it harder to communicate effectively*
> - *Be clear and ask questions if you have any suspicion that you've been misunderstood*
> - *Avoid using aggressive language and tone - it's harder to repair a remote relationship after an outburst*
> - *If it's feasible, try to meet as many of your team possible face-to-face at least once*
> - *Use Active Listening – make sure you listen, understand and remember what is being said*
> - *Study Nonviolent Communication as an effective means of communication*
> - *Use humour carefully – it may at best fall flat and at worst offend.*

Respecting different cultures

While you might feel more at home with people from your own cultural background, the research shows that teams profit from their diversity

Remote teams are increasingly becoming global. I've worked in a team who were spread across North, South and Central America, Europe, Asia and Australasia. Many big companies have offices in several countries and even small ones are becoming increasingly more distributed.

In an ever more global business community, project teams can be assembled from talent pools located all over the world so it's important to understand the issues as well as the advantages that working with such diverse teams can bring.

We often take for granted the way we communicate with one another. So many aspects of the way we interact with people, address issues and make decisions are based on our cultural upbringing. In a multicultural team how everyone communicates is critical and can be the difference between a successful team and one that finds it has more differences than things in common.

Positives

While you might feel more at home with people from your own cultural background, the research shows that teams profit from their diversity. It makes sense that a team with a greater diversity of ages, skills and backgrounds is likely to bring more to the party than one consisting of people who all have a similar outlook on life. Scott E.

Page, professor and director of the Center of the Study of Complex Systems at the University of Michigan has demonstrated that more diverse groups outperform like-minded experts[7]. He concludes that 'progress depends as much on our collective differences as it does on our individual IQ scores.'

"Diversity is good. Pass it down."

Enterprises large and small can gain positive advantage from developing intercultural expertise. Not only does this help them run more effective and innovative teams but it also empowers them to interact in a more self-assured way with suppliers, customers and prospective customers wherever they're located in the world.

Five rules

When working with individuals and teams from different cultures it's important that you:

1. Recognise the existence of different cultures and act on this

2. Be open minded, respectful and tolerant

3. Understand and acknowledge any difficulties in communicating

4. Address language difficulties directly

5. Consider developing a rule book.

Recognise the existence of different cultures

The single biggest mistake you can make is to assume that everyone you work with worldwide is going to respond well to your usual style. To do this is to run the risk of alienating any members of your team not from your culture.

There is huge variety in the way people communication worldwide with many cultures for example putting a higher emphasis on non-verbal communication. Western European and English speaking cultures tend to place a stronger emphasis on verbal communication whereas Asian, African, Arab, East European and Latin American cultures have a tendency to make more use of non-verbal cues. Claire B. Halverson in her book Cultural Context Inventory[12] describes the former as Low Context Cultures and the latter as High Context where non-verbal factors such as voice tone, gestures, facial expression and eye movement are far more significant. Especially in situations where you may not be able to see these non-verbal clues, it's very important that you listen carefully and ask questions to clarify.

It's very easy for difference to lead to stereotyping, misunderstanding and blame which makes it important to recognise this and replace conflict with empathy and understanding. If you're working with a diverse team then take the time to research the basic dos and don'ts for other cultures. Also bear in mind that it's rarely as simple as deciding how you should treat someone based only on their cultural background and from what region of the world they originate. People from the same country can find lots of differences and similarities in for example gender, race, education, religion, cultural upbringing, social class and social outlook. They may also find that the things they have in common such as a love of sport, music or movies transcends all of their differences and cements a bond. I've met a number of Indian nationals in my working life and although we haven't always had that much in common, once we start discussing cricket all of the differences fall away and we're suddenly talking a common language. Effective Multicultural Teams by Claire Halverson and Aqeel Tirmizi[13] as the title suggests is a specialist study of this and is an excellent read.

A few years ago I ran a project in London for a Japanese company. Taking the trouble to read a book on Japanese culture was not only a fascinating insight into a different culture but also paid dividends for the project and in particular helped us to successfully negotiate with our client in the knowledge that the Japanese approach to negotiation differed significantly to that used in Western Europe. Research does pay off!

Even the simplest communication can be misunderstood, for instance 'Yes' can be a dangerous word. In some cultures it means 'I agree' in others 'I heard what you just said'. There's a world of difference between those two and the wrong understanding could be disastrous. 'No' can be just as tricky. In some cultures including my own, people avoid saying no out of politeness. It seems very direct to say no, so they try to soften it by phrases such as 'I don't think it's right for us at this time' or 'I'm not sure that will work but we'll think about it' and then hope the topic never resurfaces. Non-verbal assent and disagreement can also be misleading. If you see a nodding head on a video link in response to a question, you might assume that means 'yes' but in some parts of Greece, Serbia, Bulgaria and Turkey, a nodding head means 'no'[11].

In some cultures there is a strong desire to please authority figures so people find 'no' hard to say. I was delivering a back office IT system for a company in England a while back. We were using a software company in India to deliver the system. As we approached our first delivery I kept asking them if they were on track and was constantly given reassurance that everything was going well. With our User Testing systems and team all ready to go, we received a call early in the morning on delivery day saying they'd be three weeks late. They'd been so desperate to tell us what we wanted that they had literally worked day and night to deliver and finally gave up early in the morning on the day it was due for delivery. Ten out of ten for effort, but zero out of ten for trust. With a greater appreciation of the Indian culture at that time, we would almost certainly have seen a better outcome.

Be open minded, respectful and tolerant

What might seem fine in your culture might be seen as odd or rude in another. There are lots of examples of this from blowing your nose in public to a variety of hand signals (we won't go into that!), toilet habits, and even the way you laugh.

Customs and habits differ from one culture to another. Some people habitually talk at a high or low volume. Some may be more direct or more reserved in showing emotion. Employees in some cultures have a need to exhibit a high degree of presenteeism or at least not leave the office before their boss does. Some are keen to display a high work ethic and others appear more laid back. There are all sorts of assumptions that you might make about these behaviours based on your own cultural background which may turn out to be well wide of the mark. So you need to be open minded and respectful. We tend to lack awareness of our own biases and it's easy to place stereotypes and cultural assumptions on others. Just because it seems a bit strange to you doesn't mean it's viewed the same way in another culture.

You also need to be aware of hierarchies. How senior are the people you're interfacing with? What are their expectations of how you'll interact with them according to their business and social hierarchy norms?

Attitudes to gender and age differ around the world. In your culture men and women may communicate equally with each other, but you may have to interact with people from a tradition where men have a more dominant role. In many cultures age has an exaggerated importance and deference is to the oldest person in the room. This may result in resistance to a younger person taking the lead. What you can do is to make sure you introduce yourself fully so people understand who you are and where you fit in.

In some environments senior managers are addressed as 'sir' in others this would be anathema both to the person addressing them and the senior manager.

None of these issues are insuperable, but it's important you understand them and work with not against them. In a pressured environment it's easy either deliberately or out of ignorance to impose what you see as normal on everyone else because you think that's the best way of reaching the finishing line.

Understand and acknowledge any difficulties in communicating

If you were unable to understand someone or think that they didn't understand you then it's important to say something about it. Many people find this situation slightly embarrassing especially where the individuals involved have different native languages. Asking multiple times for clarity does feel uncomfortable, but don't worry. As long as you avoid being rude or offensive, but patiently explain what the issue or misunderstanding is, you'll be ok. It's nearly always better to be open than to let a problem in communication go unaddressed and potentially lead to bigger issues later.

There are some social routines that are universal in every culture. In normal conversation these rely heavily on non-verbal feedback. Is someone upset with you? Do they feel unappreciated? Are they fed up with you interrupting constantly or being unable to listen? Face-to-face they may tell you these things straight but more likely it will be written all over their expression and body language. You may not be able to see or sense either remotely, so err on the side of safety. If you think you've caused upset, better to over-compensate than just charge on.

Thank people for work they've done. Whatever people interpret from your other actions and dialogue, it's impossible to mistake a thank you. Saying thank you is important in teams of any composition but really makes the difference in a culturally and geographically disparate team. Building team spirit is important and saying thank you is a big part of that.

Don't be afraid to apologise. You will make mistakes, you will make gaffes and you may well upset people. Make it very clear that you're apologising. In a remote team it's easy to think the moment has gone when you're mulling over something you said in a meeting. If you think you made a gaffe or upset someone then it's worth following it up with an instant message, e-mail or call after the meeting. I have one particularly embarrassing incident in mind where I'd managed to twice exclude a senior manager from an e-mail circulation list. This manager was in another country where deference to your manager was a very strong cultural norm. I made a brief apology in a meeting but thinking it over afterwards, it hadn't been sufficient. I should have written at that point to further apologise. I didn't and relations between us were never quite the same after that. I really had lost the moment. Don't do the same.

Listen and don't interrupt too much. Being listened to and not interrupted equates to being valued. No-one warms to someone who interrupts and doesn't listen, but you'll find that amplified if you're a voice on a conference call from a different culture on the other side of the world.

Language

In a team located all over the world, language and accents can be a real problem. The best advice is to make sure you ask if you don't understand something, but you may need to go a step further.

As described in Chapter 4 – Technology, more vendors of messaging and videoconferencing software are offering translation options and this is likely to be an area that improves rapidly with Artificial Intelligence moving into the sphere of translation. If you are having issues and you don't have translation software then you may need to include a translator in the meeting.

If you are in a role that regularly interfaces with teams who speak a different language to yours then consider learning that language. Being bilingual will also improve your employability and in all probability pay rate! Speaking two of English, Spanish, French and Mandarin Chinese with around 3 billion speakers won't hurt your career prospects.

A combination of poor sound quality and differing accents can be a real issue and one that starts to lead to embarrassment if you have to keep asking for clarifications. It's important that you tread carefully and give reasons why you're asking for so many clarifications rather than an implied 'you're not speaking clearly'. I worked on a project where a large team from all over Europe and Asia met weekly to discuss progress. One team in the Far East spoke in what to my ears was heavily accented English over a very bad line. We managed, but at times my frequent requests for repetition felt embarrassing. One way of overcoming the difficulties of understanding accented speech is to practise listening to and understanding people speaking with that accent. This may sound sort of obvious but it's backed up by research and it's something that's missed by most people. The research shows that native language listeners often have difficulty understanding non-native speakers and that the emphasis on making the communication successful is usually placed on the non-native speaker, with frequent requests for repetition or clarity[8]. So if for instance you you're a native English speaker and have a meeting with a non-native English speaking Brazilian once a week, then go to **YouTube** and search for 'Brazilians speaking English' and you'll find lots of practice material.

Avoid colloquialisms. It's so tempting to use the colloquialisms that you use in everyday speaking but this isn't a good idea. Keep your language simple, there is so much opportunity for misunderstandings. When the English talk about window shopping, they're unlikely to be talking about starting work on restoring a house and if the French say 'On va lécher les vitrines' they probably won't be out to see what the local windows taste like and yet both of these expressions mean exactly the same thing!

Avoid slang and profanity. Using slang or obscene language can make you hard to understand and may be viewed as very offensive. Slang and profanity require an in-depth understanding of a language and their meaning is highly dependent on context. The brain has to work hard when it translates and can find even the normal use of language difficult, particularly where two words sound similar. Throwing in additional challenges is likely to lead to confusion, so the best advice is to keep well clear of foul language.

Understand who you're talking to

Top of your priority list is to get hold of the company's Organisation Chart. Every company has one, but sadly it's usually out of date. In one project for a multi-national company I found myself talking to people in several countries without having a clue as to their position in the organisation. Most senior managers warm to a bit of deference but in some cultures this deference isn't just preferred it's programmed in from birth. Act like these guys are junior members of your team and you're in for a rough ride.

So if you can't get an Organisation Chart or it's inaccurate then use **LinkedIn**, the company's website or just ask people. Company e-mails usually contain a signature which may give a good idea of status, notwithstanding the tendency in big companies for everyone to claim they're some sort of manager. If their local guys are showing them huge deference and you're treating them as an equal (or less!) then they may find this undermining and irritating which ultimately will damage to you.

National characteristics can be misleading. For instance to most Americans and Europeans, many Indians sound very polite and deferential. Given the cultural norms in Europe and the US and the sort of personality that manages to climb the greasy pole, there's a natural tendency to view someone who comes across this way as being less senior. That would be a very big mistake to make. To a British ear the way that many Americans express themselves may sound brash and confident, maybe even a little intimidating, but actually they're just as full of uncertainty and insecurity as the rest of us. Don't be fooled into applying your own cultural norms to others.

Consider developing a rule book

Consider all of the points made above and think about developing a rule book or training or both.

The tendency is to wait until something goes wrong before putting rules or training in place, but with the sort of issues raised in this section it's entirely possible that you won't discover any damage until it's too late. It's easy to get a bad reputation, difficult to lose it. Don't set yourself up for a fall through lack of thought or ignorance.

> **Key recommendations in respecting other cultures**
> - *How well everyone communicates in a multicultural team can be the difference between a successful team and one that finds it has more differences than things in common*
> - *Take the time to research the basic dos and don'ts for other cultures*
> - *Be open minded and respectful.*
> - *Keep your language simple and straightforward and avoid colloquialisms*
> - *Use **YouTube** to practice understanding accents*
> - *Avoid slang and profanity. Using slang or obscene language can make you hard to understand and may be viewed as very offensive*
> - *Thank people for work they've done. Whatever your cultural background it's impossible to mistake a thank you*
> - *You will make mistakes and you may well upset people. Don't be afraid to apologise*
> - *Think about developing a rule book or training or both.*

Country specifics

Language, time zones, working hours and legal variances all add to the challenge

Language and time zones

Make sure you have a plan for handling language differences. As mentioned earlier the software market is moving towards providing language translation in videoconferencing and instant messaging and decent services already exist for document translation. However if you don't or can't have automated translation facilities then consider how you are going to compensate. Do you need to employ a translator? If so has this been allowed for in your costs and how easy will it be to find someone who may need to have technical skills or understanding in the area you're working in as well as a fluent command of two or more languages?

Time zones can be a real nightmare. Just try arranging meetings (as I have) between three people, one in Europe, one Australia and the other in the Western USA. There's no way you can do this and not have someone working in what would either be their sleeping or leisure time.

Working hours

While working hours tend to extend or become distorted particularly if you're working across time zones, there may also be more fundamental differences in working hours.

The local working day can vary across the world. Countries within the same time zone may have differing working hours depending on how close they are to the equator. Work in hotter countries tends to start much earlier in the day and finish in early afternoon or be split by a long midday break when the sun is at its hottest.

The working week may differ too, for instance while Europe, Japan and the US work Monday to Friday, much of the Islamic world works on Sundays but not on Fridays.

Public holidays will vary both in their frequency and place in the calendar. I worked with a company in the US who seemed a bit shocked by the number of public holidays Europeans had against the very few that they had. This can make things difficult and can also result in pressure on you to appear at meetings that happen to fall on public holidays in your country.

There may also be times of the year when staff may be thin on the ground. School holidays in the UK start in July and continue until early September. Most employees with children will take a two week vacation during that period. This is the case in many countries, but of course the dates will differ. You need to be aware if key staff are planning to be on vacation just when you're most likely to need them.

Legal restrictions

What's legal in your country may not be legal elsewhere. For instance I was working with an application that we had installed right across the world but found because of variance in data protection laws, there were some countries where we were unable to deploy it. Once again it's a case of not making assumptions. Ask questions early and avoid these sorts of issues later.

Key Recommendations in Country Specifics
- *Make sure you have a plan for handling language differences*
- *If you're working across time zones you're going to have accept an increasing blurring of work and leisure hours*
- *Be aware of differences in working hours and days and times of year that resources may not be available in other countries*
- *Be aware of legal differences. What's legal in your country may not be legal elsewhere.*

4
TECHNOLOGY

Technology overview

The technology needs to facilitate both collaboration between members of a team and the co-ordination of the team by a manager

There is a host of technology available to facilitate remote working and it's an area that's experiencing explosive growth. The two words that cover the technology are collaboration and co-ordination. It should facilitate collaboration between members of a team and the co-ordination of the team by a manager. The market is positively overrun with a wealth of tools that will allow you to achieve both collaboration and co-ordination of geographically dispersed teams but very few that hit everything you're going to need in a single package.

So how do geographically dispersed teams work together? Well they're going to need some way of talking to each other, so that's where videoconferencing comes in. They might need to send messages to each other, so e-mail and instant messaging is useful. They'll need to share files so some sort of shared workspace is pretty handy and as importantly share knowledge on a searchable knowledge base or wiki. Finally the team will need to co-operate and work to plans which is what project and task management software is designed to facilitate. The good news is that all of this is well provided for by a wide choice of software vendors. The bad news is that there are an awful lot of them – project and task management package vendors alone run into hundreds and there are growing numbers of instant messaging and videoconferencing packages to choose from. However, both storage for shared workspaces and knowledge base tools are fairly mature markets where making a choice should be reasonably straightforward.

If you thought all of that sounds challenging, once you start looking a bit closer you find that there is a huge degree of overlap between these tools. Many task and project management packages provide chat boards, instant messaging and shared storage and have very close integrations with e-mail. Many of the videoconferencing packages include chat and many of the instant messaging applications are also set up to facilitate topic or project based chat boards.

My feeling is that longer term, mergers and partnerships will result in a consolidation into a single market for 'collaboration and co-ordination' tools which will include shared spaces, task and project management, instant messaging, chat boards and videoconferencing. The big vendors like **Microsoft** and **Google** are already moving solidly in that direction.

The main consideration for the selection of any package should be best of breed. As things stand, you are likely to find that buying one package for collaboration and co-ordination won't work because the one that does everything isn't best of breed for any one aspect of its functionality. Comprehensive and least worst might not be what you're after! However if you've already invested in a package from one vendor then you may be tempted to buy the rest from them too. This is likely to be the simplest approach but not necessarily the best or most future-proofed.

This chapter is organised into:

- Communication Technology – covering videoconferencing, messaging and e-mail

- Project and Task Management Tools – a description of what types of tools are available and what they'll do for you

- Buying Project and Task Management Tools – what features to look out for when buying one of these tools

- Shared Workspaces – cloud based file storage

- Knowledge Bases and Wikis – searchable databases of knowledge

Communication technology

A good videoconferencing set up is a key factor in productivity and teamwork in a distributed team. Every dollar spent on videoconferencing is money well spent

Introduction

In this section I'll cover videoconferencing, instant messaging, chat boards and e-mail. As mentioned earlier a lot of this technology has overlaps. For instance most instant messaging software tools provide chat boards as well as voice and video messaging. Videoconferencing software usually comes bundled with instant messaging. Your main concern should be to source the best of breed in each category and make sure that each package you buy has a good level of integration with everything else.

"It's too late! Bob's brain has been sucked out by the internet!"

Videoconferencing

The proliferation of employees occasionally working at home combined with headsets and webcams appearing at nearly every desk gives the management of most companies the belief that they are set up for videoconferencing. It's also common to see rooms set up as videoconferencing rooms with just a hi-res camera and a couple of decent microphones. In the most basic sense these facilities can be used for video meetings but if you want videoconferencing to really work, you'll need to do a lot better than this.

I can't stress enough how important a good videoconferencing set up is to productivity and teamwork in a distributed team. Every dollar spent on videoconferencing rooms is money well spent and the more you spend the better your communication will work. Good videoconferencing kit includes a smart camera that zooms in on the speaker – not just one that shows a wide view of the room where you can barely make out faces. It has high resolution cameras, and screens and good quality sound. Just about every software vendor will support 1080p high resolution images but the some will give you 4K resolution which provides stunning video images. When you use these facilities you feel like you're talking to a real person and not to a grainy image of a room with some anonymous people sat in it. This is important, humans are built for social interaction and to pick up subtleties of body language and facial expression. In many of these facilities, this is totally lost.

While there is a proliferation of videoconferencing software, it all does pretty much the same job. Each of the packages has strengths and weaknesses but the biggest difference you'll make to the experience is how much you invest in the hardware. Good quality cameras are a little more expensive but are vastly superior to the cameras built into laptops and webcams selling for $30 or less. They will produce good images even in low light, include autofocus, have a wide field of view and are able to zoom in or out without losing quality. The better webcams will have dual microphones and capture good quality sound. If you look on Amazon and you'll find a huge choice of webcams, but personally I wouldn't look further than **Microsoft**, **Logitech** or **Poly** and don't go for the lowest priced models.

Videoconferencing requirements for internet bandwidth aren't arduous but remember that if you're sharing a line with other users then your broadband speed will drop significantly. Because of the way videoconferencing works both download and upload speeds are important. You should have at least 2 Mbps download and 1 Mbps upload speeds to get a decent connection with 1080p resolution. This bandwidth requirement does increase slightly the more users you have on a call but this shouldn't be an issue unless you're using **Skype** which has been described as being to video conferencing as a go-kart is to a sports car and does use more bandwidth the more participants you have on a call.

In a recent role I hosted a weekly meeting with invitees from eight countries. We used **Zoom**, but it could have been just about any desktop videoconferencing package. Given issues with bandwidth we had to cut the video to get decent audio reception. In addition I had to have the sound on maximum to just about work out what the representatives from some countries were saying. This wasn't a great medium for getting stuff done with the poor technology putting a dampener on any real sense of interaction.

I worked for a bank who subcontracted work to an IT company in India. We spent the first six months of the work speaking to the supplier on telephone conference calls. The lines were poor and so was the equipment being used and the results were terrible. I was losing patience with and confidence in the supplier until we installed a good videoconferencing facility. Suddenly I was talking to real people not some distant voice on a phone and our relationship and understanding was transformed. This is a particularly important concern for companies who are doing business around the world. Good videoconferencing facilities will help with selling, supply and support.

Videoconferencing is absolutely key for geographically dispersed teams. Often quite complex work is distributed across a team in different locations. In this environment the communications software has to be a facilitator not an inhibitor.

Content sharing and white boards

All videoconferencing packages incorporate screen sharing but not all allow you to share a single window or application rather than the entire screen. Being able to share a single window reduces the chance that you'll accidentally broadcast something you don't want the whole meetings to view. You may be thinking 'so what?' but accidentally broadcasting commercially sensitive or private information could land you in a whole heap of trouble.

If you're in the creative industries and find whiteboards useful then there are plenty of vendors who support shareable interactive white boards which try hard to replicate the meeting room experience.

Of course if you've purchased a camera with a wide enough field of view and that has zoom capabilities, you can share an actual whiteboard rather than a virtual one.

Webinars, training and recording, break-outs

With companies and employees becoming more distributed, videoconferencing has become an increasingly popular tool for webinars and company Town Hall meetings. Many sales organisations like to use webinar facilities to sell to new clients and engage existing ones. If this is important to you then find out if the videoconferencing tool supports these and in particular how many concurrent users are supported.

In a similar vein, you may want to use videoconferencing facilities for remote training and learning. This should be a very similar set up to running webinars.

You may also be able to make use of break-outs in both training and webinars. This gives the person who calls the meeting the facility to set up virtual break-out rooms with two or more attendees from the main meeting and then have them rejoin the meeting at a later point.

You should also look at the recording facilities offered. As well as being able to record Town Halls, training sessions and live webinars for distribution and later viewing, it can be very useful to record contractual discussions or to be able to provide customers with a recording of a demo by videoconference.

Mobility and voice-only

Many videoconferencing packages support a variety of devices from desktop PCs to mobile devices including laptops, tablets and smart phones. These devices are likely to run a variety of operating systems and variants and versions of those operating systems. This can become quite complex as many tools want to download a desktop client or browser add-on for the best quality, security and flexibility. This is fine as long as it works on all of your devices and browsers. If you need to support a wide variety of devices then check that at a minimum the videoconferencing software will work in a browser without an add-on and check which browsers and versions it supports. There's also nothing worse, and I've experienced this myself, than arriving on time for a meeting, trying to log into the meeting only to find out the videoconference you've been invited to uses a package that wants to download software on to your computer. After ten minutes and a lot of fiddling around you finally make the meeting, late and in a newly wound up state!

If your team is mobile as well as remote then it may be important to be able to include a participant in the meeting who is travelling. Voice-only is likely be very important in this respect so that participants can dial into the meeting using conventional telephony.

I have several times been involved in meetings where at least one participant was in their car and dialing in hands-free. Maybe not the best idea for safety but it's a useful facility for busy people and particularly where people are working in different time zones when your midday might be in the middle of someone else's commute. The dial-in number should be toll-free regardless of what country the person is calling from.

Quality

Quality is king in the videoconferencing world. Get the best quality videoconferencing set up that you can afford.

Desktop licences for videoconferencing packages like **Skype for Business/Microsoft Teams, Zoom, Lifesize, Bluejeans, Lark, LogMeIn, Cisco Webex** and many more are relatively cheap and a high quality webcam, speakers and/or headset won't set you back very much either. Camera/screen resolution should as a minimum support 1080p but you may want to consider 4K. Most new laptops have 4K capable screens.

If you're going to set up videoconferencing facilities in house then look at companies like **Poly** (formerly Polycom) and **Logitech** who have been in the business of improving video and audio conference quality for decades. They existed long before the current proliferation of desktop software packages were even imagined. Their systems integrate with the leading videoconferencing software packages so you can run videoconferences with people coming in from multiple sources. These set-ups better emulate a meeting where everyone is around a table in the same room. The smart cameras provided will rotate and zoom in on the person talking rather than hearing a voice emitting from a distant video of a group huddled around a table. Every CEO should have this quality of facility in their office. If you're having trouble convincing your management to spend money on better quality facilities, then set up a side-by-side demo and the objections will quickly fade. Entry level systems aren't that expensive, so please have a look at what is available.

Administration and Reporting

Most packages offer reporting for call, device and feature usage and quality of service performance. They'll also provide a detailed breakdown of usage by user.

There are a variety of set-up options available in different packages. Some e.g. **Lark** use voice recognition to provide subtitling. It's common that the software switches the screen to the person talking but some offer that as an option. Pretty much all offer recording as an option but not often with their free versions. Some e.g. **Zoom** provide accessibility features to vary the on screen font sizes. If virtual backgrounds turn you on then that's a common feature too, done particularly well by **Microsoft Teams** right now. Having your video window always on top is also a nice feature if you're say working through a problem on a call and need to flit around other windows to find the solution. Several e.g. **Cisco Webex** provide this.

Videoconferencing package vendors

There is no shortage of videoconferencing packages. These come from suppliers who have started from different places in the software marketplace. Some are selling office applications and have added videoconferencing into their collaboration toolset e.g. **Microsoft Skype/Teams** and **Google Hangouts/Meet**, some from communications companies e.g. **Cisco** and **Arkadin** (NTT) and some from smaller, more agile and innovative players in this market e.g. **Zoom, Lark** and **LogMeIn, Lifesize** and **Bluejeans**.

Be aware that the larger players are trying to tie you into their complete office or communication suites and so are a lot weaker on integration with other collaboration and coordination software whereas by necessity the smaller companies will put greater emphasis on offering a wider range of integrations.

A number of vendors offer free use of their packages on a reduced functionality, limited meeting time and/or limited user basis. This is of course an attempt to get you hooked before upselling you a more performant version.

If you are looking for a free package, as things stand at the publication of this book, **Lark** is the best deal currently going with almost no limitations on the size and length of meetings. Lark is a bit more than just a video conferencing package and includes messaging, e-mail integration and cloud storage in its free version. **Jitsi** is interesting too, it's a totally free open source package which is rated very highly for quality and security and can support up to 75 attendees. **Lifesize** and **Google Hangouts** aren't far behind with no limit on the duration of meetings but a limit of 10 participants. **Cisco Webex** offers 50 minutes free for up to 100 users and **Skype** has no limit on duration for up to 50 users, but to be honest I'd find it very hard to recommend Skype which is falling well behind the rest of the market.

As with many of the other tools we've looked at in this book, there is a proliferation of vendors in this market and some of the smaller ones clearly will not survive or will be gobbled up by other players. While videoconferencing is important, it's probably a little easier to change should your current vendor go out of business than to change your shared storage or project management package. Even so please check the financial status of the vendor before signing up.

Please check the minimum bandwidth requirements for internet upload and download for your package. These aren't generally arduous but they differ from vendor to vendor and if you need to set up videoconferences where one or more of the participants has poor line speeds then this may be a consideration.

Instant messaging

Instant messaging is everywhere. WhatsApp on mobiles has become the world's favourite instant messaging app with over 1.5 billion users at January 2018 and 65 billion messages sent every day. It probably isn't the greatest tool to use for a project team but the principles it works on are not so different to business messaging applications. At a basic level they all support one-to-one chats, group discussions and the inclusion of a wide range of media into the chat stream.

You can see how useful instant messaging can be from the widespread use of WhatsApp by consumer businesses as well as by individuals. Want to get a dent fixed in your car? Just send the dent specialist some images of the bent panel by WhatsApp and they'll send you a quote without ever having seen your vehicle. Web chat buttons are appearing on lots of websites to help customers to resolve issues or queries and I find them more responsive and a lot less irritating than picking up the phone and having to listen to some inane imitation of music for 10 minutes before I get to talk to someone. Instant messaging applications are also starting to invade the world of medicine with a boom in applications that connect you via a mix of messaging, voice and video to a medical practitioner.

Instant messaging can tie a geographically dispersed team together day-to-day and hour-by-hour. You have to be careful it doesn't become a time consuming distraction, but used properly it's a way of resolving issues quickly and keeping a team communicating.

Business messaging applications usually support a wide range of integrations with office, video conferencing and other third party software and the smarter instant messaging applications are moving towards mixing chat, chat boards, voice and video all in the same package. Can't quite work out what someone is getting at in a text chat? Click and have a quick one-to-one audio or video chat with them. This helps gets around one of the biggest irritants with remote working which is not being able to have a quick chat to clear the air or sort out an issue. The type of thing that in an office environment, you'd walk around to their desk to sort out.

The better tools allow you to put a hold or bar on incoming messages for a defined period so you don't have to be plagued by people who want to talk while you're getting on with something that you need to dedicate your full concentration to.

As with all collaboration and co-ordination tools the market is exploding with packages. There are the usual suspects **Microsoft**, **Google** and **Cisco**, but other new smaller players like **Slack**, **Twist** and **Discord** are starting to gain a real foothold. Of these Slack is the one that has the biggest profile and say they processed 1 billion messages per week in 2019, however Discord which is open source and license-free claims to be processing twice as many. Discord came out of the gaming community and isn't quite so business focussed as Slack. Twist is a genuine competitor to Slack. Of the three Slack has far more off the shelf integrations available including links to e-mail, storage, videoconferencing, project management and programming applications.

Make sure your instant messaging application facilitates group chats as well as one-to-one messaging and that the messages are stored and are both searchable and archivable. Most instant messaging applications also allow you to organise messages by topic, interest area or department similar to chat boards. The facility to produce a transcript from a chat meeting is also useful.

You should be able to load or link to files into your messages and ideally to invite other users of your messaging application in other departments or companies into your message threads.

On the security front, a number offer password protected group chats if you're worried about someone breaking into a group. Messages should be encrypted both in flight and at rest.

Messaging is pretty handy for maintaining communication wherever you are, so it's very important that a business messaging package works on a wide variety of devices – from desktop PCs to tablets and mobile phones.

As mentioned earlier most of the messaging applications overlap with the other collaboration and co-ordination tools which may have messaging and chat boards already built in. Many are free to use but charging starts either once you exceed a number of users or exceed a storage upload limit. Another common limitation with the free versions is to severely restrict access to your message history. Licence costs are relatively small and charged per user per month for packages hosted in the cloud, but check how much storage this gives you. While chat itself uses very little storage, videos, images and documents included in the chat do, so make sure you won't be hit for an additional charge if you exceed a storage allowance.

E-mail

E-mail has been with us since the 1970s and isn't about to disappear just yet. It will remain part of the suite of communications tools for some time to come. E-mail overload is a common complaint and tends to get worse if you're working remotely. There are some developments that may help with that.

Automation is becoming more available through packages like **MixMax** which can be set up to automatically schedule meetings, tell you who's read an e-mail you sent and remind those who didn't that you're expecting a reply. **MixMax** also provides you with a variety of e-mail templates to hopefully help save you time.

A number of the collaboration and coordination tools integrate with e-mail. For example it's common for task and project management packages to send e-mail reminders for tasks to be completed and messaging applications often have tight integration with e-mail.

Language translation

I was working recently with a distributed team made up of native English, Spanish and Portuguese speakers. Our conversations were technical and detailed and proved so difficult that eventually we decided to bring a translator into the meetings.

The good news is that this doesn't have to be the case as suppliers are starting to provide the option of language translations in videoconferences, instant messages and chat board applications. The translations are never going to be perfect but should convey the gist of what is being said. If this is important to you, you may want to trial tools that offer this.

Security

A lot of potentially confidential and/or commercially sensitive information is going to be communicated via the public internet, so instant messages need to be encrypted in transit and your voice and videoconferencing should conform to the current security protocols. You may also want to consider using a Virtual Private Network (VPN), there's more on this in Chapter 5 – Security.

Many videoconferencing and instant messaging packages offer password protected meetings and message groups. If security is a concern then don't buy a package that doesn't provide some sort of meeting ID and a separate password. Don't send people links that bypass the need to include a meeting ID and password, it's too easy a route for intruders to infiltrate the meeting.

Security is important for videoconferencing. The absolute must is end-to-end encryption of video and audio. Most but not all vendors support this. Don't invest in a package that doesn't. **Cisco Webex**, **Skype** and **BlueJeans** all provide end-to-end encryption. Most videoconferencing applications will show who is attending a meeting and some offer the meeting host the facility to mute, block or drop attendees from a meeting and to lock the meeting once everyone has arrived. Look also for packages that play a sound when someone joins or leaves (to avoid unauthorised attendees slipping in unnoticed).

There has been a lot of recent publicity regarding back doors into videoconferencing software allowing hackers to gain control of your computer's camera. This shouldn't be facilitated by any software package. Make sure you probe your supplier closely on the level of security and vulnerabilities in any packages you're looking to buy.

No-one thought too deeply about security when e-mail was invented in the 1970s so one of the downsides with e-mail is that it isn't secure. You may want to invest in a secure e-mail service like **Posteo** or **ProtonMail**.

Hosted or on-premise

All vendors offer a hosted service but you may be interested in running videoconferencing and instant messaging on your own servers for performance or security reasons. In this case ask vendors if they support an on-premise deployment, that is one that you deploy on your own servers or data centre.

Key communications technology recommendations

- *Get the best quality videoconferencing set up that you can afford*
- *The software is pretty much standard, the hardware makes the biggest difference - buy good quality cameras, sound and screens*
- *Instant messaging can tie a geographically dispersed team together and become a way of resolving issues quickly*
- *Take a look at e-mail automation*
- *Consider a secure e-mail service*
- *Look for communications packages that integrate easily with each other and other elements of your IT infrastructure*
- *Language translation will improve dramatically as Artificial Intelligence advances further into the world of language translation*
- *Make sure messages are encrypted both in transit and at rest and that video conferencing is encrypted end-to-end*

Project and task management tools

Project and task management tools have proliferated in recent years. These tools allow you to manage and organise work wherever those carrying out the work are located

Introduction

Until quite recently selecting project management software was something a 10 year old could easily have done. A very small market was dominated by **Microsoft Project** with few alternatives available other than resorting to pen, paper and a ruler. Those days are long gone, with a flood of project and task management packages coming into the market. At the last count more than 400 packages were available from as many suppliers, resulting in a complex, crowded marketplace.

IDC a global provider of market intelligence, advisory services, and events for the information technology sector forecasts that the global market for project and portfolio management tools will grow at 6.8% per annum from around $4.5 billion in 2017 to $5.7 billion in 2022.

So how do they help manage remote work?

If you're running a remote team there are three ways to manage the work:

- Do nothing and hope everyone gets stuff done

- Organise your work into projects and plan and monitor them
- Carry out task management on a week to week basis

With the exception of the first bullet which isn't a recommended approach there are a multitude of packages available that will do some or all of the remaining two.

The packages that support task management are effectively simple workflow solutions. You set up a workflow – sometimes as simple as assigned, in progress and completed, assign tasks to individuals and monitor their progress. The project management packages are more sophisticated allowing complex plans to be put together and tracked. There are some basic requirements regardless of the approach taken. You're going to want to share plans or workflow with your team members. You'll probably also want them to be able to log the time they've spent on work and how complete they think their planned activities are. You'll probably be competing for resources with other groups in your company so need some way of managing the availability of resources. You're likely also to need to produce reports for management.

Pretty much all of the available project and task management tools are designed to allow you to manage teams regardless of where they're situated. Most also facilitate communication with and between team members through message boards, comments on tasks and instant messaging and allow the sharing and review of documentation, images, graphics, video and audio. Better still, many will allow you to share plans with your customer and produce reports virtually at the click of a mouse.

The more sophisticated packages are backed by a relational database, which allows you to use commercially available data analysis tools to show any aspect of the work being managed in easily understandable graphical summaries. The right tool will also provide an executive level view, to be able to run reports that show at a glance the status, financials and delivery dates of work being carried out right across a department or company and track performance against original estimates. If you're a project based service company, you'll be able to monitor revenue and profit for each of your projects and for your entire project portfolio on a week-by-week or even day-by-day basis which gives you a high degree of control over your business.

Ultimately they should save you time and help you be more organised and co-ordinated. However, initially you'll need to invest time setting up resources and templates, training staff, understanding the full capabilities of the package, and agreeing standards for how you're going to use it.

Project based service companies

I'd go as far as saying that this sort of tool is absolutely essential if you're running this sort of business. You'll be able to monitor your profitability and identify your major financial risks on a week by week basis. You'll know which projects look likely to overspend and which ones look like they'll make lots of money. You'll have a week by week view of your employee utilisation, a vital piece of data for any resource based business. More than that the package will impose its own discipline on your employees. Project managers will need to keep their plans up to date and team members their time logged. If they don't you can see it all instantly on the reports you can get from these systems.

There are countless examples of project based service companies getting into trouble with underperforming fixed price contracts. It often seems hard to believe that these companies could have allowed so many contracts to get into difficulties. The better project management tools put company boards back in control. So if you're running a project based service business this sort of package is an investment you'll never regret.

Cloud based

All of these applications are available as a service via the cloud, so you don't need to buy any special infrastructure, just pay your subscription, point your browser to the right place and go. Most vendors also offer collaboration space in the cloud, where plans, documents and other files can be shared and reviewed and team members can communicate.

Another common theme in this market is that like most cloud based software, these tools are subscription based. This is usually by a monthly charge although most vendors want you to sign up for a minimum of a one year term and either make this a contractual requirement or offer you a considerable financial incentive to do so. Nearly all vendors offer a free 14 or 30 day trial and some a totally free limited functionality configuration of their package as a taster to tempt you into their paying versions.

All of the packages will give you access through a browser and many through a mobile app, allowing you to access tasks, plans, data, time sheets etc. through pretty much any device at just about any location. Some vendors also offer on-premise versions for you to install in your datacentre or on a server. On-premise gives you added flexibility and security and it's also not uncommon to see vendors offering wider functionality for on-premise versions than the hosted versions. You'll usually pay a one off license based on the number of users and an annual maintenance fee thereafter. But also be aware that in some cases there may be an additional service charge to ensure your installation is kept in line with the hosted version.

Not a single market

There are a variety of packages out there. Some try to be all things, some to carve out niches. But as a general rule I'd split the market into 5 sections:

1. Specialist Agile Tools

2. Task Management Tools

3. Standard Project Management Tools

4. High End Project Management Tools

5. Large Enterprise Level Tools.

In case you haven't heard of it, Agile is a methodology used primarily by IT teams to develop software in a more flexible, user focused way. The Agile tools are tailored to that methodology and while it is possible to use Agile for any application, it is predominantly used for IT projects. These tools are specialised for that market but vary from cheap tools that can maintain a backlog and support running sprints to comprehensive tools that support running a portfolio of Agile projects. Examples of Agile tools are **Jira**, **Axosoft**, **Assembla**, **Target Process** and **Spiraplan**.

The Task Management Tools are as the name suggests aimed primarily at task management. Most offer some collaboration functionality and in fact many are collaboration tools with task management glued on. Most will also allow you to build workflows of varying levels of sophistication. There is a very wide variance in price for this class of tool, but that variance isn't always reflected in delivered functionality. Examples of Task Management Tools are **Asana**, **Basecamp**, **Monday** and **Trello**, but **Jira** also appears in this camp as it can be used for task management as well as for Agile. Many of these tools have an open architecture and encourage third parties to build add-ons to expand their core functionality.

Standard Project Management Tools support all of the functions you would expect to see in a project management package plus pretty much everything normally provided by Task Management Tools. They all have capable task management, all support Gantt views, all allow time recording and most will show actuals against estimated. They all have decent reporting and most support financial reporting and invoicing. Again the variance in price in this class of tools can be dramatic. The other thing to note about the better tools in this market is that they're for obvious reasons trying to match the functionality of the high end tools without creeping too far into their pricing range, so some real bargains are available here. The sort of tools I'd classify here are **EasyProjects**, **Wrike**, **Liquid Planner**, **Smartsheet** and **Zoho Projects**.

The High End Project Management Tools support everything you get in a standard tool but in a more comprehensive and usually very flexible way. They will often include the ability to build processes and to capture and manage risks and issues and track change. These tools will support your business regardless of what size it grows to. Some are tailored to specific businesses e.g. service companies, some are more suitable for in-house teams. Most are moving to storing all project data in a relational database and offering Business Intelligence (BI) tools to provide sophisticated graphical reports from this data. They are just below the Enterprise Level Tools sold by the likes of Oracle and Hewlett Packard, but not by much. Once again pricing can vary dramatically, without any real increase in value. The sort of tools I'd classify here are **Microsoft Project Online**, **Cora**, **Mavenlink, KeyedIn** and **Clarizen**.

Enterprise Level Tools are costly and aimed at very large companies. These packages are more likely to run on a large company's own IT infrastructure than in the cloud and are highly integrated with other tools provided by that vendor. Examples of these are **Hewlett Packard's PPM** and **Oracle Primavera PPM**.

Changing your mind might be more difficult than you think

If you're thinking because these tools are subscription based, that if the package doesn't turn out to be right for you then you can easily move on, then think again!

Despite offering a monthly subscription, more and more tools are mandating a minimum one year term, so you'll be committed to a whole year's outlay. This isn't a nasty sales trick, it's mainly because of the overheads involved in both setting you up and maintaining you as a new customer on their hosted service. It's also because in an increasingly competitive market vendors are finding they need to sign you up for a year's subscription to cover the cost of their sales effort.

Most of the Standard and High End Tools will offer you a start-up package. This involves analysing how you do things now, configuring the package to your needs and then training your employees in this configuration. This is a great idea. I've come across a number of companies who thought that buying a project management package would solve all of their delivery problems and then sadly found it made virtually no difference. It isn't just about the package, it's also about how you use it and the processes you build around it. Done well, this start-up phase will challenge you to determine how you're going to use the software effectively and consistently. However, there will be an additional one-off charge for this.

Even if you pick a low end Task Management Tool, you'll still invest a huge amount of time into making it work for you. You'll need to work out what the package can do, train staff, build standards, build plans and resource profiles into it and start filling it up with files, messaging threads and review comments. Vendors know this, which is why many offer subscription free starter packages.

It becomes a very difficult decision to change once you've purchased a package and started to use it. I've worked with companies who have purchased what have turned out to be poor value tools, with significant deficiencies, but even so were very resistant to make a change because of the effort involved and that they were simply too busy.

One of the companies I know bought a tool that didn't include employee time tracking, so rather than change to a package that did, they found it less hassle to buy a separate time recording system and then try to link them together. Another struggled with the way the package scheduled activities and found that it didn't support the notion of a fixed price project very well, which given they were an IT shop, wasn't great.

It's easy to be critical but it really isn't easy to get this right and you're likely to be committing to a significant investment once you add the start-up charges to the annual fees and training time for your own staff. These are complex pieces of software, so take your time choosing the right package for you. Get your due diligence right. You might want to think about trying to find a consultant who knows this market well to help you through this stage of the process. A couple of months spent deciding what you want, looking into the detail and checking out a few packages will save you a lot of money and heartache later.

Key project and task management tools recommendations

- *Its very difficult to run a remote team well without using one of these tools*
- *Task management tools will allow you to manage tasks and simple workflows*
- *Project management tools allow you to organise tasks into projects and plan and monitor them*
- *Changing is not easy once you've started using a tool, so take time and care to carry out due diligence and pick the right package*
- *Most tools are cloud and subscription based but if it's important to you, on-premise versions are available from many vendors.*

Buying a task management or project management tool

The most important factor in buying anything is to be clear what your requirements are. Get your selection right – choose in haste and repent at leisure!

Introduction

The most important factor in buying anything is to understand what your requirements are – you wouldn't be at all surprised if you ended up buying the wrong package if you didn't know what you wanted in the first place. This is especially true if you haven't used a project or task management tool before, when as often happens in that scenario, you'll end up learning the hard way. This is a complex market place with hundreds of tools available with a wide range of capabilities and as explained earlier buying the wrong tool will be a costly mistake.

Is the vendor here to stay?

Before you start looking at features and functionality, you need to ask a few questions about the potential supplier.

As we've already pointed out, you'll find that project and task management software isn't just for Christmas, it's for life. Once you start using a package you swiftly become inexorably tied to it. So there are two imperatives:

- Get your selection right

- Pick a product that is going to be around as long as you hope your business will be.

With more than 400 suppliers out there, the only thing that is certain is that a lot of these are either going wind up out of business or will be gobbled up by their rivals. What seems probable is that the poorer tools, the ones currently overcharging for their delivered functionality and the ones with a low installed base are the most likely to disappear as market growth tails off. Many vendors are also supported by venture capital and don't have a viable business as yet.

So the important questions are:-

- What is their installed customer base?
- How long they've been in business?
- Can they show you financial results and employee count for the last five years or if not how they are being financed?
- Can they provide you with reference customers with a similar profile to you who you can contact?

Another consideration should the worst happen and your supplier goes out of business is that you still have access to the data that you've stored in the package. Check this out before buying.

How do they support the package?

You'll want to know what standard of support you're going to get once you've purchased the package. Where is support located and what hours and days of the year do they provide support? If they're on the other side of the world, they could be in bed just when the package starts crashing or you desperately need some help to complete a plan for a client. How do you contact support? Is this by logging a support ticket, sending an e-mail or by phone and what sort of response times do they quote for each? Don't underestimate how important one of these packages could become to your business, particularly if you use them to manage tasks or workflow across a large dispersed team.

Price also comes into this and as well as being related to the functionality of the package is also going to be reflected in the level of support. If you're paying $30 per user per month expect better and more responsive support than if you're only paying $7.

Hosting

All of these packages offer a hosted service, so find out how this is going to work. For a start make sure you're clear about any limitations on storage. Can you have unlimited tasks, projects and files or will your monthly charge be increased once you breach defined storage limits?

All of your plans and files are likely to end up being held on a remote server, so you need to know about back-ups and disaster recovery. What happens if there's a flood or other sort of disaster at your supplier's hosting facility? How long will it be before access to your plans and files are restored? All vendors should have a disaster recovery strategy. Their servers will also be down for routine maintenance at various times, find out when these are and what the historic uptime has been for their facility. Most vendors will use one of the big hosting service suppliers such as **Amazon AWS** or **Microsoft Azure**, but be aware that these hosting suppliers offer a wide range of differently scoped services. Find out what service your supplier has purchased and if it addresses the back-up and disaster recovery concerns we've detailed above.

Performance of the application will also depend on what level of service the package supplier has purchased with their hosting provider. The CPU and disk capacity purchased and the degree of sharing with other users of the hosting facility will affect performance and can cause frustrating delays and time lags.

You may for reasons of performance, control or security want to have the package run on your own infrastructure. Not all vendors support this, but you will find many who do. You may also find you have to pay an additional support charge to keep your version in line with the cloud version.

Browser and operating system support

Think about how you want to access the software. Check that the browsers, browser versions and mobile devices that you want to use are supported. If Apps are available for mobile devices, will they be supported on the operating systems you want to use? Often only a subset of the package's overall functionality is supported on a mobile device. If mobiles are important to you check what functionality is supported on what platform.

Security

This system may hold the keys to your business or a significant part of it. Documentation and plans for all of your future developments are not the sort of thing you want falling into the hands of your competitors, so you should be concerned about security.

Most vendors offer encryption of data in transit, but fewer offer encryption of data at rest. Usually your data is held in a shared instance in a server farm which may not meet your security needs. If it doesn't then ask if you can have your own encrypted instance, but be warned this is usually very expensive and it may be more economic to host the package yourself.

Permission levels are another must-have. You're going to need to be able to define a number of roles with different permissions e.g. Administrator, Manager, User, Customer. Some packages come with set roles, others let you configure role types from a large set of permissions.

You may also want to know about log-on security. Phishing is the single most effective hacking technique. You might want a package that offers two-factor authentication and/or enforces a change of password at defined time intervals. Check what the package's password and security policy is and if this is configurable.

What features do you need?

Clearly it's a good idea to decide what you need before going out and buying anything. With something as feature-rich as task and project management packages, you would do well to decide not only what you want now, but also what you think you may need in the future.

Many vendors up-sell features on the basic subscription, so be careful you don't buy something that appears to be good value, but turns out not to be when you find you have to pay an increased subscription for something you need. While the package should be easy to use, I'd also advise not to get seduced too much by a flashy look and feel. Functionality will help you run your tasks, processes and projects, not the way it looks. As we've already said, features don't necessarily equate to price. Some packages are ridiculously overpriced for the functionality that they deliver. Make sure you're paying for the features being delivered, not the vendor's large advertising budget!

Bernard had a unique but effective Project Management style

Gantt charts

Nearly all tools will also show you a list of tasks and most but not all tools can produce project plans as a Gantt chart, the ubiquitous bar chart representation of a plan, invented by Mr Gantt in the 1920s. I wouldn't feel I had a project plan unless I could see a Gantt chart with resourcing, deliverables and dependencies. If you're the same make sure the packages you look at support this.

Dependencies

Being able to set up dependencies between tasks is very important to be able to schedule them properly. Dependencies are a bit more complex than you might at first think. You should be able to make another task dependent not only on an earlier task finishing, but also on that task starting and be able to offset both, that is 'start task x, n days after task y has started/finished'. This allows you a lot more flexibility than the simple 'start this task when that one has completed' type of dependency that you find in most packages.

Constraints

Constraints are handy and add more flexibility to how you can construct your schedules.

There are a number of possible constraints, but the most important ones are:

- That an activity must start by a given date
- Or must end by a given date
- Or must start no earlier than a given date
- Or must finish no earlier than a given date.

Examples of how these would be used are:

- Start by a given date might be used for a seminar, where publicity has gone out and speakers booked, so the 'run the seminar' activity must have a fixed start date, which would also affect the dates of preceding activities
- 'End by a given date' might be used if you know that the only resource with the skills to carry out this activity is about to

leave the company or be assigned to another department, so you need to have the activity completed before you lose them
- 'Start no earlier than' is mainly used where there are dependencies on external activities or resources e.g. a supplier completing work that you are dependent on. You may not have to start on a set date, but you know you can't start until the external dependency has been fulfilled
- 'Finish no earlier than' is used in situations where you know a task has to be completed, but you also know there's no rush, so you can use this to schedule it for when it's needed, which might help you with resourcing it.

Levels

In your business you'll probably have a top level of clients or business areas and then projects/tasks below that. If you're managing projects then they themselves will then probably break down into sub-projects and tasks. You need your software to be able to support this sort of structure.

Resources

You need to be able to put resources into your tasks and plans and you may want to add both a cost and a charge rate to each resource. The cost rate for a resource won't vary but the charge rate may well do, so ideally the charge rate should be variable by project and/or customer account. This will allow you to calculate what each piece of work and your portfolio of work is costing and if you're a service company whether you're in profit or not.

All packages will allow you to allocate employees to your tasks and plans but with some you can also include physical resources e.g. the costs of renting a building, buying a computer or a software package.

You might think that resourcing is just about allocating free employees to tasks, but it's much bigger than that. You may need to be able to see who is free when across the whole company resource pool, find resources with the right skills and make sure they're not over allocated once you've assigned them to your tasks. For this, you need to have the ability to associate skills with resources, so that you can look for a free resource with say copy writing skills. You also need a portfolio view so that you can see at a glance which resources are free at what times across the whole company resource pool. With this information you might talk to another manager to see if a resource you need could be spared for a couple of weeks by adjusting their plans or alternatively move an activity in your plans to accommodate when a resource is free.

You probably want to be able to look ahead to see when resources become free to make sure you're not going to have people sitting around waiting for suitable work. If you're running development shop then you really want to know when pools of resources, say designers, developers and testers are likely to be over or underutilised so that you can optimise their use. If you're a service company, keeping the utilisation of resources high will ensure a healthy bottom line. Having people sitting around is bad for morale and bad for your profit margin.

Scheduling with project management tools

First let's deal with auto-scheduling. By this I mean that a change to project x will automatically change the schedule for project y, if a resource needed by both projects is extended by project x. This is showing the effect in real life, clearly if Bill is wanted by both projects and Bill is extended by project x, then project y can't have him, so it will slip. However this can make it quite difficult to disentangle what has happened, particularly if several projects and several resources are involved. If I'm running my project particularly well, I'm likely to be a bit shocked when my schedule extends because of something that has happened on another project. It can take significant time and effort to work out what has gone on, especially where several projects and resources are involved. Clearly the overuse of a resource needs to be flagged up, but the alternative is for the project/task management software to indicate that the resource has become overloaded so that in the example, both managers see that some action is required. The managers can then find out why the resource is overloaded and try to sort out the issue. Both have their pluses, but I wouldn't recommend selecting a package that only auto-schedules. I'd look for one that gives you an option to switch auto-scheduling on or off, to allow you to decide what works best for you. In the end you want to be in control of who is scheduled to do what and when.

Reminders

Most packages will send out e-mail reminders to staff regarding their current and forthcoming tasks. This reminds staff that they have tasks to complete this week and more tasks coming up the following week. This is a nice facility, but be careful you don't use it as a substitute for talking to people! It's also easy to find in-trays filling up with reminders, particularly for staff who are working on lots of tasks, so look at how this function can be configured.

Status reporting

It's important that reporting is done frequently and early, otherwise you can end up finding something is amiss when it's too late to do anything about it. One of the real positives with project and task management packages is that all of the data is held in the tool, so it's usually easy to produce reports from it. The quality and breadth of the reporting tends to distinguish the better tools. Reporting can take up huge amounts of your time. Good project and task management packages should make it easy.

The trend for the better packages is to store all of the data they capture in a relational database so that you can use a Business Intelligence (BI) tool to produce whatever reports you want in numerical or graphical format or both. The power of BI tools is that they allow you to drill down into the data. So for instance a summary showing all work in the portfolio would allow you at the click of a mouse to drill down into an individual project or department performance or the performance of all work for one customer or by one team. A resourcing view of the entire resource pool would allow you to drill down by skill groups, teams or individual to determine when resources are free and which resources are being over-scheduled. You'll usually be provided with a library of predefined reports but after that it's up to you. This is a very powerful and flexible tool allowing you to analyse both individual projects or sets of tasks and the entire portfolio of work.

Capturing time and spend

A large number of packages offer nothing more than scheduling. They'll let you set up task lists and a Gantt chart and assign resources to tasks, but that's about where it ends. If you're going to be able to track how well your work is doing and in particular what you've spent then you need to be able to capture time. This is typically done by providing an online timesheet for individuals to record what time they've spent on what activities. An important feature to look out for is approval of this time. Lots of packages only allow the entire timesheet to be signed off by a nominated approver. In the better packages, the manager of each piece of work signs off the time that individuals have spent on their work. This is much more empowering because as manager you may want to question people's time entries or challenge an entry in error from someone who doesn't even work for you.

You may also have a need to export timesheet data if you have a customer who wants you to re-enter time spent on their work into their time recording systems. This isn't an uncommon requirement for a service company.

Risks, issues and actions

Monitoring risks, issues and actions are some of the most basic and important jobs that a manager needs to carry out. Some packages include being able to register and monitor risks, issues and actions. I wouldn't see this as a high priority requirement, more a nice to have, but it's good to have all of this information in the same place rather than in a collection of spreadsheets.

Integrations

All of the Enterprise Level Tools include integrations with other software. These tools are aimed at large corporations with considerable investment in IT infrastructure so this is clearly important to them, but you may also find this of value to your company if for example you want to link to your accounting software to track spending or produce invoices.

Many packages offer integrations to popular software like QuickBooks and Salesforce and most offer an open API (Application Program Interface) which can be used to build an interface with almost any other piece of software, but make sure if you have particular integrations in mind that the vendor can give you guarantees that you can connect.

In addition many of the Task Management Packages and some of the Standard Project Management Packages have open architectures where they encourage third parties to produce add-ons to their core software. The Task Management Packages tend to have smaller core functionality and then a whole host of add-ons available to both enhance the functionality and interface to other software. A good example of this is **Jira**, which is a simple task management package. You can buy add-ons for Jira from countless vendors for workflow automation, project management, time recording, invoicing, test management and asset management as well as a whole host of integrations. There are literally thousands of add-ons for Jira. Jira is low priced and the add-ons generally even cheaper or sometimes free, but there is a risk of ending up with a complex array of tools from different vendors that don't work quite as well as a single integrated package. Support can also get tricky where a number of vendors are involved. The Standard Project Management packages tend to be far more feature rich so their add-ons are fewer and focussed on interfacing. A good example of this is **Wrike** who have less than 50 add-ons which are primarily integrations with office applications, storage providers, e-mail and CRM systems.

Workflow

Nearly all of these packages have some level of workflow. Tasks are assigned to individuals and given target end dates. Individuals see a queue of tasks waiting for them and a manager can both deal with the allocation of tasks and monitor progress. As a minimum tasks can be viewed as 'assigned', 'in progress' and 'complete' and can be set up to have dependencies on each other to provide a complete workflow. Many packages will provide even more statuses to describe the workflow, like 'requested', 'in review' or 'stuck'. Most of the Task Management Tools will work well if you want to manage a team via workflow rather than the potentially more complex set up of a project.

Tools like **Jira** and **Trello** can provide more sophisticated workflow through the third party add-ons they offer and in addition you might want to look at dedicated workflow packages like **ProofHub**, **Filestage** or **Swiftcase**, but these tend to be aimed at specific industries like insurance or marketing and facilitate complex create and approval workflows.

Dashboard

Most packages provide each user with a summary dashboard with their tasks, their outstanding actions, reminders, risks and so on. However some packages only give this view and don't allow users to see the entire plan unless they have project manager privileges. This matters if they charge more for users with project management privileges, as several vendors do. **Microsoft Project online** is an example of this. The basic user license doesn't cost a lot but allows only a very limited view of the project plan. Look out for this, it's definitely not helpful for users to only be able to view a small portion and not the entire plan.

File storage

Many packages include a built-in file repository. Most will support links to a variety of external file stores e.g. **Google Drive**, **Microsoft SharePoint**, **Dropbox** and **Box**. Where a file repository exists it may also support version tracking, that is if you modify a file or upload a new version the package automatically saves the old version. This provides you with security in case someone messes up the current version and an audit trail of changes made to a file.

Portfolio management features

Portfolio management is one of the huge positives with using project or task management software. It will allow you to:

- Monitor progress and costs for your whole company
- Utilise staff efficiently
- Forecast your ability to bid for or start new work
- Know what your entire portfolio of work is costing you
- If you're a service company to understand the revenue and profitability of your entire project portfolio on a week-by-week basis.

Given all of the data for your work is held in a single package, producing reports for portfolio management should be easy, although it's not uncommon for suppliers to charge more for their reporting suite. As mentioned earlier, more and more suppliers are now moving to an architecture where the data being gathered by the project/task management package is stored in a relational database and reporting carried out using a BI tool. The supplier will usually provide a set of prebuilt reports so you can either modify the existing ones or build new ones according to your need.

This is a very powerful facility at the portfolio level. You could for instance produce reports which show your revenue and profitability by project over time, so you can look at the trend of what happens to your projects. If they all start profitable and start to lose money somewhere around testing then you can build an action plan to resolve this. You might want to show the loading of your team over time and by groupings. This would allow you to see that say your copy writing or programming groups start to fall off a cliff into zero utilisation in a couple of months and that you'd better do something about this. Reporting using BI tools is such a powerful feature that it will help you run your business. You can monitor the profitability of your entire portfolio week-by-week or if you're an internal department track against budget, without even opening a spreadsheet. More than that, once senior management are used to seeing this level of reporting then lax processes lower down the food chain will become immediately apparent. This forces managers to keep plans up to date and team members to fill timesheets in on time, which can only be good.

Collaboration features

More and more tools place an emphasis on collaboration, so as well as being able to share plans and files, to provide discussion boards, instant messaging and the ability to review and comment on documents. One of the strengths of this is that discussions and review comments which usually end up in long e-mail or instant messaging trails are saved within the project/task management package in an orderly, accessible and searchable format. It also provides an audit trail that makes it easier to track decisions and settle any disputes you might have with suppliers or customers.

Training and user guides

Training is important. These packages are complex, even the lower priced ones. Don't underestimate how much effort it will take to get everyone up to speed. You also need to think out how you're going to use the package in your business rather than just diving in and getting on with it. You need to think about what you want to get out of the package. Do you have to produce invoices? If so what data needs to go into them and at what level of granularity? Do you need to report on progress or on spend? Do you have an existing project management or task management process that you want to reflect in the package? How do you want to capture chargeable and non-chargeable time? How do you want to show vacation and how do employees book this? These and more will have a big influence on how you set the package up. You need a set of rules and more often than not the best approach is to talk to the supplier and get some training, rather than blundering on thinking you're saving yourself money by doing it yourself and having to sort the mess out later.

Many vendors will combine an on-boarding and training package and you'll pay a one-off charge for this. On-boarding isn't necessarily simple. You might have data to transfer from the software you're using now and most of these packages are highly configurable and need to be set up appropriately for you. Also take a look at the user guides and videos that come with the package. The best packages will have simple, searchable reference guides and short videos on the stuff you commonly need to do.

Pricing

Well the good news is that pricing starts at zero, but before you get too excited, you should note that vendors aren't charities. The strategy for many vendors is to start you off at low or no cost with a version of their software with limited functionality and then upsell when you inevitably start to find that you need to do more. Remember what we said earlier, once you start using one of these tools in anger, it becomes hard to move away. Suppliers know this. Going for the cheapest package before looking closely what it delivers is highly likely to be a waste of time and money.

The free or trial versions give you the opportunity to evaluate one or a number of packages to determine which is the right one for you. In an evaluation it's important you're clear about what you want to get from a package and try to attach priorities to your requirements. Make sure you don't try to evaluate too many packages, get down to a shortlist of three or four. When you decide which one best meets your requirements I'd strongly recommend you then try to use it with some real work. It's only then that you start to clearly identify any issues or omissions.

Pricing is often on a per-user basis, but sometimes charging is by active projects. You need to decide which model works for you. Be careful to ensure that any features that you've assumed are included for free really are included. It's common to charge extra for a BI package and for integrations with other software. Storage may be limited too. This can all result in the costs increasing dramatically above your initial assumptions so check what you're going to get for your money.

Key considerations in buying a project management package

- *Be clear what you want before you buy*
- *Is the vendor here to stay? What is their installed base? What is their financial position?*
- *Is your data secure? Does the package support encryption of data in transit and at rest? Do they support a password and security policy and SSO?*
- *Who owns your data? Make sure it's you and not the vendor*
- *Look for Gantt charts, workflow management, Kanban boards, dependencies, constraints and multiple levels*
- *Make sure you can manage assignment and scheduling of resources*
- *Can you capture time spent on tasks?*
- *Producing reports should be easy. Packages with a relational database and a BI tool offer the most comprehensive and flexible reporting and analysis*
- *What integrations are supported? Integration with an accounting package or other collaboration tools may be important*
- *Does the tool allow you to manage and monitor portfolios of work?*
- *How good are the training and user guides and what will start-up cost?*

Shared workspaces

It's very difficult to make any team work without the ability to easily share files. For a team who are geographically dispersed it's just about impossible

If you're going to collaborate effectively then you'll need to share workspaces to allow you to make the variety of materials produced available to the whole team.

If you decide to go with the suite of office, collaboration and co-ordination tools available from bigger suppliers such as **Google** and **Microsoft** then most of this can be delivered in a reasonably integrated way from a single supplier. However by doing this you'll have to make compromises and it's unlikely you'll be sourcing the best of breed for each category of tool. In fact if one of the bigger suppliers manages to launch the best of breed package in every category then everyone else may as well pack up and go home, but usually this isn't the way things work. If you are sourcing a variety of tools from different suppliers then you'll get some shared storage with each tool. Messaging tools will have their own space, so will task and project management tools and videoconferencing packages. Because of the way these tools work, much of this will be transparent but what is essential is that each of the packages you choose interface with each other and in particular with your shared storage provider.

Storage

There are countless cloud storage vendors from the huge and impersonal giants to small enterprises offering a more personal and potentially cheaper service often using a chunk of someone else's server farm. Popular and well established vendors are **Box, Dropbox, Google Drive, Microsoft OneDrive** and **Amazon Drive** but you might want to look at smaller companies like **Syncplicity, Tresorit** and **OwnCloud**.

Pretty much all of these vendors will offer a facility where a local drive or file is synced to cloud storage. You can then modify either the cloud version or the local version and the changes will be reflected in both. However this can result in a 'last user wins' situation where if you change your local copy of a file, when it syncs with the shared version you may end up overwriting someone else's edits. This is more a document management system than true shared storage. The ideal in shared storage is where a shared document can be edited by several parties simultaneously and still maintain its integrity. This is true document sharing, often referred to as co-authoring and reflects the capabilities of the editing tools more than the storage provider. For instance the online versions of **Microsoft's Office** tools support co-authoring and so does **Google's G-Suite**. **Microsoft** and **Google** both allow you to co-author using **Box** and **Dropbox** as your file store as well as with **OneDrive** and **Drive** respectively. Neither Microsoft nor Google support co-authoring on each other's storage.

Security

Your storage is likely to contain commercially sensitive documents so you should be very concerned about its security. You should be looking for encryption both for data in transit and at rest. Most suppliers will provide this. You should also be concerned about how individuals gain access to the data. Ideally you'll have an SSO (Single Sign On) set up with the same security co-ordinated across all of the products in your collaboration and co-ordination suite. If you're not using SSO then you should look for vendors who offer multi-factor authentication and the ability to set a security policy e.g. forcing users to change passwords at a defined frequency and password composition rules.

Some of the smaller storage providers use security as their USP. For instance **Tresorit** promote themselves as 'the most secure cloud storage' and **sync.com** strongly promote their security credentials. Files are encrypted using a security key. Both Tresorit and sync.com provide zero-knowledge encryption which means they do not store a copy of this key. This means you and only you can decrypt your files. Both also offer two factor authentication and a host of other security options. Sync.com's servers are in Canada who have one of the most stringent privacy regimes in the world. Tresorit allows you to decide which country you'd like your data stored in so you can choose the jurisdiction that suits your needs best. If bulletproof security is vital to you then take a look at these providers.

Back-up and disaster recovery

If you don't want to run the risk of losing data, then you'll want your shared workspaces to be backed-up. So check what's included in the price. Is a weekly back-up sufficient for you? Some vendors will back-up on the fly, so any loss of data, accidental deletion etc. will be retrievable pretty much instantly. Can you specify your own back-up schedule and how easy and fast is it to retrieve old back-ups? Find out what your provider's back-up policy is and how flexible it is.

Be aware that the vast majority of data loss is caused by human error and while the back-ups carried out by your storage provider may cover that for a short period this will not be for ever. For instance deleted files on Google Drive and OneDrive go into their respective recycle bins. Google Drive automatically empties this bin after 30 days and OneDrive after 93 days. Once that has happened your file is gone for good. If this concerns you then you might want to look at a specialist back-up solution such as those offered by **Backupify** or **Spinbackup**.

You may also be interested in versioning. This allows you to access previous versions of a file, giving you an audit trail of what has been changed and the ability to correct an erroneous or unintended update with minimal fuss. Many suppliers provide document versioning.

Disaster recovery is also very important. How would your business be impacted if the facility where your files are stored flooded or suffered a fire and was out of action for a week or longer with no access to your data? You probably don't want to take such chances, so enquire about your vendor's disaster recovery processes. You should expect a back-up held off-site as a minimum and ideally that there is a hot standby facility so should the building where your files are held disappear into a hole in the ground, an instant switch is made to a geographically distant facility with minimal disruption. Instant switching is becoming more common given how easy it is to replicate servers over high speed data connections.

Multi-platform

Many storage providers work hand in glove with desktop based operating systems, so the cloud storage just appears as folders in a user's local storage. This is very slick and easy to use, but it may not necessarily work on every operating system in your network.

There's also no reason why your shared workspace shouldn't work with mobile devices. If this is important to you make sure that Android and iOS devices are supported.

Key recommendations in shared workspaces

- *The simplest form of shared storage is where a local drive is synced to cloud storage. However this results in a 'last user wins' situation and is less shared storage than document management*
- *The ideal is that one document can be edited by several parties simultaneously -* **Microsoft Office** *and* **Google G-Suite** *support this with several shared storage providers*
- *Look for encryption in transit and at rest.*
- *Look for two-factor authentication to beat phishing and implement SSO*
- *Is versioning provided? This gives you an audit trail of all of the changes made to a file*
- *Understand the vendor's back-up and disaster recovery procedures*
- *Is the storage accessible from all operating systems and mobile devices?*

Knowledge bases and Wikis

Sharing knowledge is a great idea regardless of the location of employees. For a remote team it's a big productivity aid to know you can find the information you need instantly

One of the downsides with remote working is you can't ask the guy next to you or the one in the next office or your manager to answer a quick question. Total frustration sets in when you try to call or message the person you think might have the answer only to get a reply four hours later suggesting you ask someone else!!

Knowledge bases and Wikis are a way of helping make life a bit easier. Both are searchable databases of knowledge. The difference between the two is that usually anyone can contribute to a Wiki but only authorised users can contribute to a knowledge base. A knowledge base needs an administrator and tends to be more organised but a Wiki needs little or no administration. Wikis are very commonly in use by teams of IT programmers and IT support staff. Find something weird with the Java Compiler that took 2 hours to sort out, drop the solution into the Wiki. Find a hard to resolve issue with one of the systems that you're supporting, write that up in the Wiki too. IT is full of weird faults arising in complex set-ups and complicated ways of setting a system up. Once you've fought your way through that you really want to write it down so you know how to fix it next time. A Wiki is perfect for this. The main downside with a Wiki is that it can get overloaded with information and worse still, loaded with garbage, so it often can be hard to see the wood from the trees. When you search a Wiki and get a huge number of matches then it's getting too unwieldy, but you can control this if you manage your Wiki and put rules in place as to who can do what.

Lots of companies use Wikis to hold corporate information – everything from HR policies to how to claim expenses, book travel and hotels etc. If the content is controlled it's easily searchable and allows remote employees to find out what they need to without chasing around to find the person who knows. There are a huge number of free Wiki's available or you can buy one on a subscription basis, hosted in the Cloud. Some of the better free Wikis are **Confluence**, **DokuWiki**, **MediaWiki**, **Xwiki** and **Wiki.js**. Confluence is hosted and free up to 10 users. Xwiki can be downloaded free or paid for hosted. Other than Confluence, they'll all take a bit of setting up and none come with support.

If you want something that will require less effort from you and is better supported then you could go with a hosted Wiki. Some of the better ones are **Confluence**, **Xwiki**, **ZoHo Wiki**, **Papyrs**, and **Nuclino**. Most have free options to get you started with either limits on space or users or both. There are also a number of providers who specialise in hosting Wikis, so you could choose to have any of the free Wikis hosted on one of these. Take a look at **SiteGround** and **A2Hosting** if you want to take this approach.

Knowledge bases take the Wiki concept one step further. The aim with a knowledge base is to make all of your company's data searchable and accessible in a way that facilitates employees' productivity. Examples of these are **AllAnswered**, **Bloomfire** and **Helpjiuce**. Searches and analytics are far more sophisticated than for a Wiki, results more graphical and often Artificial Intelligence is deployed to find the answer you want rather than lamely showing you every hit on a search term. Given any employee might have contributed, the data in Wikis isn't always either accurate or well written. They're company versions of Wikipedia with the same pluses and minuses. Knowledge bases typically contain data only from Subject Matter Experts, are read-only for most employees and should score high marks for accuracy and credibility.

> **Key Recommendations in Knowledge Bases and Wikis**
> - *Both are searchable databases of knowledge*
> - *Both make life a bit easier by providing access to company-wide knowledge and other employees' experience in solving issue you might discover*
> - *Wikis are for everyone to update and read and are usually cheap to buy and set up*
> - *Knowledge bases are usually only updated by subject matter experts and are more expensive to buy and set up. They generally have more sophisticated search facilities*

5
SECURITY

The biggest issue

Poor security can destroy the credibility of a remotely run team and it's important to understand that it's as much about how people act as it is the technology

Arguably security is the single biggest issue in remote working. When security comes to mind we tend to think about firewalls, encryption and secure connections but security is as much about the actions of the people on your team as it is about the technology.

In-house security teams concern themselves with all aspects of keeping a company's data and processes secure. This ranges from IT security and vetting of employees to the locks on the front and back doors.

Once the front door is opened and the operation spreads to potentially anywhere in the world then security risks are bound to increase.

Technology

While of course technology is the enabler for remote working, it's also a source of vulnerability. Remote employees could be using insecure Wi-Fi, computers with poor security or lose mobile devices containing sensitive information

Technology allows us to achieve stuff we'd never dreamed of even ten years ago and it is the principal enabler for remote working.

Remote working revives a whole lot of familiar challenges, many of which have already been fixed in the in-house working environment where removable storage is usually banned and Wi-Fi is encrypted and secure. Remote resources could be working in cafés or other public areas with little or no security. They might lose mobile devices containing sensitive data. This all presents a much greater challenge for security officers than the comforting office environment does.

VPN and VDI

A Virtual Private Network (VPN) can be viewed as a secure encrypted pipe running on the public internet through which you can channel some or all data transmitted between one point e.g. a laptop computer and another, likely to be a server. VPN is readily available and relatively inexpensive. It means that wherever the employee uses their computer, laptop or mobile device as long as they access the cloud application via VPN their connection will be secure.

Signing up to a VPN provider or configuring your own VPN set up in-house is one of the best steps you can take to ensure security for remote workers and make certain that data will be far more secure in transit. It also allows you to build a secure link into your in-house applications, e-mail and secure servers. You can even provide some or all of the applications available on your in-house desktop to remote workers using VPN. However this is a two edged sword, while it provides a secure method of remote working, it also opens a back door into your network, so you need to ensure that users who log on to the VPN are fully authenticated. VPN also doesn't stop users downloading potentially sensitive data to their devices or uploading viruses from those devices to your network. To remedy these issues, you may wish to hide some parts of your network from remote access, protect the VPN with a firewall and ramp up your monitoring of miscreant activity.

Because of the way VPNs work they will inevitably slow things down but this isn't likely to be an issue other than for very high bandwidth applications like videoconferencing. The most important factors will be your proximity to the VPN server and the number of simultaneous users of that server. As with most things, you get what you pay for, the cheapest VPNs are likely to be the slowest. Before signing up for a VPN find out if you will take a performance hit from introducing it. There is no shortage of business VPN providers. **Perimeter 81 Business**, **NordVPN Teams**, **Encrypt.me** and **VyprVPN** are all good VPN providers right now.

The gold standard for secure remote access is to provide Virtual Desktop Infrastructure (VDI). This means that each desktop is running either in the cloud or on an in-house server sitting behind your firewall. The remote worker then connects to their desktop via the internet. No applications are run locally, no data is held locally and you can enforce virtually all of the security policies that you run in-house. VDI requires a lot of hardware centrally and has a high maintenance overhead so is relatively expensive, but if security is very important to you, this is the ideal set-up for remote working. VDI has been around for a long time with **Citrix** and **VMWare** two of the most established players in this market. Most of the big hosting providers e.g. **Amazon AWS** and **Microsoft Azure** will facilitate VDI in the cloud.

Even the best security will be hard pushed to completely stop employees or contractors from being able to download, e-mail or instant message files from your network or from shared storage to computers with poor security. If you want to try to close this gap there are a variety of tools like **Teramind** and **Clearswift Adaptive DLP** that can be used to identify and secure sensitive data in your network and monitor suspicious activity such as download or e-mailing of that data. Ideally highly sensitive data, such as customer information should never be open to access by remote workers, but in some circumstances e.g. remote call centres and customer service centres this is unavoidable. In these cases the software being used needs to be carefully designed to both keep data secure in transit and to limit the potential to be able to screenshot or photograph customer data.

Applications in the cloud

So while a VPN is secure, cloud application providers are also improving their act in terms of security. Encryption in transit and at rest isn't everywhere yet but it's spreading fast and will soon be a hygiene factor for all business cloud applications where security is important. If employees are accessing communication and coordination software in the cloud then make sure the level of security provided by those applications is good. This is covered in detail in Chapter 4 - Technology.

"We'll never guess her password."

Sign on

Phishing is the easiest way for fraudsters to gain unauthorised access to applications and data. It is a form of fraud where the hacker masquerades as a reputable entity and tries to induce their target to reveal log on details, usually via a link embedded in an e-mail or text message. You'll probably have received a few e-mails like this in your private e-mail box. Politicians have recently been the targets for this with phishing being used to harvest e-mails which are then leaked at election time. However this is easily prevented with two-factor authentication. There are lots of different ways of achieving this from hardware token devices which require the user to enter a code to apps on mobile phones which produce a numerical or QR code to a simple text message via a mobile phone. Check your software supplier supports two-factor authentication. Ideally you should provide a Single Sign On (SSO) with two-factor authentication for your entire remote environment but the individual packages you buy will need to support SSO.

Many organisations find it a challenge to keep track of individuals working for them particularly where contract or temporary resource is concerned and where existing employees change roles. This becomes a lot more challenging when a large part of the workforce is remote, distributed around the world and likely to be on flexible contractual terms. Good Identity Management becomes important both to track who has access to what and to pick up when employees leave the company.

Information security

You'll probably be storing a whole lot of your valuable data in the cloud including plans, message history, chat boards, webcasts, recordings of meetings, training videos and project documentation. You may have a variety of different suppliers for this using different hosting providers. As mentioned earlier make sure each of these suppliers have adequate back-up and disaster recovery procedures and that contractually you're the owner of all of this data. If you use portable devices such as tablets and laptops it's prudent but expensive to supply every remote worker with an encrypted laptop to your company's standards. This guards against a security breach caused by someone leaving a laptop on a bus or train.

People

The single biggest security risk in any enterprise is the people who work for it.

You can have secure and encrypted messaging and videoconferencing but if an employee allows someone to read the messages or overhear a meeting then all of that encryption is useless. Most videoconferencing and messaging applications allow guests to take part. In a previous role I used to attend a videoconference meeting with around 20 participants, internal and external to the company. In addition sometimes deputies turned up. It was often difficult to be sure that everyone at the meeting was supposed to be there. Adding to the confusion was the tendency for people to turn up late or leave before the end.

So be careful that everyone at your videoconference is permitted to be there. This is unlikely to be an issue if there are less than six of you but this can be a definite risk for larger meetings. If someone is trying to meeting-jump they're more likely to do it once the meeting is underway and everyone is distracted. There are options to help you block this. Most packages provide a waiting room facility where the meeting owner has to specifically admit each participant to the meeting and you can turn a sound on for when each participant joins. Some videoconferencing software also allows you to lock a meeting once it is underway. You might want to consider this for larger meetings where you're not familiar with all of the participants. It might also encourage people to arrive on time!!

Videoconferences and messaging should be password protected and you should never send out a link to a meeting which removes the need to enter ID and password. Many videoconferencing packages offer this facility for ease of use but don't use it, it offers carte blanche to someone who wants to sneak into your meeting.

There have been a number of incidents recently where a press photographer has managed to capture an image of a printed page of notes that a politician or one of their aides is carrying, revealing embarrassing detail about what they had been discussing behind closed doors. In a videoconference a high definition camera might well capture private or commercially sensitive information, so take care that the camera is capturing your face only! To facilitate this, many videoconferencing packages allow you to blur your background or replace it with an image. The same goes for screen sharing, it's very easy to reveal something you didn't want to if you share the entire screen. Many videoconferencing applications give you the option of sharing an application or window rather than the entire screen. If not then close anything sensitive before you start the videoconference.

For maximum security the meeting host should have control over who screen shares – most videoconferencing packages provide this option. You also need to be aware if you're recording videoconferences that the recording could go anywhere once you've let a third party download it. This could be dangerous if say you revealed commercially sensitive information in the process of a sales call or were talking about something you wouldn't want to be made public. So don't record videoconferences as a matter of course, let all participants know when a meeting is being recorded and make sure you store the recordings securely where only authorised users can access them. If you are distributing recordings then be very careful that they do not contain anything that you wouldn't want to be made public.

Remote access security audits

Periodic audits provide an assurance that the right level of security is both in place and being maintained for remote working.

Given the security risks inherent in remote working, it makes sense to carrying out periodic audits of all aspects of your remote set up. This should cover not only the technology but also the rules in place and practices being followed by remote workers. This is sometimes referred to as Remote Access Penetration Testing and it is usual to ask independent security experts to carry this out.

This should cover:

- Hacking. The auditors attempt to find the ways through your remote IT security set up that a hacker would use to attack your systems and compromise your security. This would include probing IT systems for vulnerabilities as well as using techniques like phishing and fraudulent contact to test remote workers' security awareness.

- Remote worker security. The auditors would carry out hacking attacks on a sample of remote workers to test the security they have in place.

- Review of the remote IT security architecture and of the practices and training provided to remote workers to maintain security.

Key security recommendations

- *Remote resources could be working in public areas with poor security and they might lose mobile devices containing sensitive data*
- *Signing up to a VPN provider or configuring your own VPN set up is one of the best steps you can take to ensure security for remote workers*
- *If security is paramount then go a step further and look at using VDI but bear in mind that it's expensive to set up and maintain*
- *Ideally customer data should not be available to remote workers but if this is unavoidable then software being used needs to be carefully designed with security a very high priority*
- *Chose cloud applications that support a security policy and two-factor authentication and SSO*
- *Be careful that everyone at a videoconference is permitted to be there*
- *Make sure that sensitive information isn't accidentally screen-shared in a video conference*
- *Use monitoring and/or have policies that forbid remote employees from downloading data on to insecure local devices or printing sensitive data.*
- *Videoconferences and messaging should be password protected*
- *Carry out periodic Remote Security Audits*

6
LEGAL POINTS

Contractual

Cover all of your legal liabilities by publishing a home-working policy

To ensure that you've covered all of your legal liabilities for home-working, I'd strongly advise you publish a home-working policy for employees and have this reviewed by a lawyer.

You'll need to consider:

- What you expect to provide to employees and what they are expected to provide e.g. computer, headset, high speed internet connection, furniture, heating and lighting etc.

- Who is responsible for insuring what equipment?

- If using their home as a base for work is allowed within the employee's rental/mortgage agreement

- If the risks associated with working from home are adequately covered within both employees and employers public liability insurance

- Expectations are set regarding remote employees attendance at meetings and with their managers either remotely, in the office or both

- Expectations are set regarding contact between employer and employee, so employees can't go off grid

- How performance will be monitored

- Do you want to have different contracts for home workers or at least ask them to sign home-working agreements?

- How IT and other support can be accessed and what hours it will be available

- Are there contractual issues or local rules that have to be addressed on working time?

- Security and computer abuse policy for home workers.

- Health and Safety requirements (see next section).

Health and Safety

In many jurisdictions Health and Safety is a legal responsibility of the employer. Make sure you assess the suitability of an employee's remote working environment

Depending on your local health and safety rules, when your own employees are working remotely you may need to assess the suitability of their working environment by carrying out a workplace risk assessment and making sure that your employer's liability insurance covers remote working.

You should also consider offering advice to employees about looking after their own health while working at home. Spending long hours hunched over a laptop or a mobile device is unlikely to be good for posture and back health. Some employers provide a workstation and chair to remote workers to avoid being subject to a legal case from an employee who has sustained an injury from working remotely.

While most employees seem to enjoy the benefits of working from home, as was witnessed during lockdowns during the COVID-19 pandemic, there can be negative effects on mental health. Increased stress can arise from 24/7 working. It can affect family life, may increase the intensity of work and blur the boundaries between paid work and personal life. It's worth considering providing advice to home-working employees regarding potential impacts on their mental health and putting in place an independent counselling service through an Employee Assistance Program (EAP).

Discrimination

Are remote employees being treated in a sufficiently different way to their office based equivalents that this could be viewed as discrimination?

Are remote employees being treated more like workhorses than their office equivalents? In some industries a disproportionate number of remote workers are female. Practice that appears to favour office based employees against remote workers by hours worked, lack of consideration for promotions and involvement in the company, while being bad practice could also lead to accusations of discrimination. You may want to consider educating managers to rule out this sort of bad practice.

Bullying and Harassment

Bullying and harassment become more difficult to detect in a remote environment, but have a corrosive effect on morale and can lead to legal action

Bullying can be an issue in an office environment, but it's a lot harder to pick up when it transforms into cyber bullying in a remote team. Cyber bullying could consist of unkind emails, frequent interruptions during videoconference meetings and overly aggressive emails or messages from managers. From the comfort and safety of their home it's easier for employees to lose inhibition and exhibit hurtful or bullying behaviour, particularly where social and work events merge in the remote social events proposed in Chapter 3 – How to Build Successful Remote Teams. With employees physically isolated from each other, doubt and insecurities may creep in and the actions of other employees, and particularly managers might be more readily misinterpreted.

Employers need to be attuned to this. I'd recommend that existing policies are reviewed and where appropriate modified to cover cyber bullying. Employees should be notified both of the courses of action open to them should they feel they are victims of bullying and of the standards they are expected to uphold in a remote working environment. Disciplinary action, if required, is likely to be a lot more straightforward in a remote environment given most interactions between employees are electronic and so highly likely to be available as evidence in a complaint or dispute.

Employers should also give thought to proactive monitoring and training to avoid incidents arising. Bullying and harassment as well as leaving companies open to legal action, have a corrosive effect on team spirit and productivity and may lead to the loss of valued employees.

Confidential Information

Beware of confidential client data ending up being printed out and used as scrap paper

Beware of the legal implications of sensitive data ending up on remote workers' computers or being printed and ending up in non-confidential waste or maybe even the remote worker's children's classroom as scrap paper!! You need policies in place to reduce the risk of this happening.

> **Key legal recommendations**
> - *Publish a home working policy for employees and have it reviewed by a lawyer*
> - *Assess the suitability of employees home working environments*
> - *Offer an Employee Assistance Program (EAP)*
> - *Make sure home workers are not subject to different treatment to office based staff*
> - *Be attuned to the possibility of cyber bullying and harassment*

7
CONCLUSION

It might even save the planet

The COVID-19 epidemic has supercharged remote working and the companies who support it. **Zoom** for instance saw its numbers of users rocket from 10 million before the pandemic to 200 million during it and its share price leap by 70%. **Slack** too saw a 40% increase in paying customers and **Microsoft Teams** an increase of 12 million users per day in March 2020. While this massive boost in use will subside, the demand for remote working will not go away.

The epidemic has incentivised enterprises to work out how remote working can be used effectively and introduced many to a work life away from the office. The rewards for companies from increased remote working are huge as long as they can build productive working arrangements and make good use of the technology. Office rental costs can be slashed, employees happier and more productive, disaster preparedness and recovery improved, plus they'll have plenty to boast about in the boost to their environmental credentials with fewer staff travelling to work. Flights, car and public transport journeys are all likely to reduce. More than that the best talent no longer has to be persuaded to up sticks and move to where a company is based but can work productively from home with occasional visits to head office.

The communication technology to support remote working worldwide is improving all of the time with more fibre optic lines being laid and the introduction of 5G cellular networks promising data rates comparable or faster than land lines without the need to dig holes and put cable in the ground. While governments around the world are restricting immigration, the remote working revolution is doing away with the need for it. The best talent can work in a remote team regardless of where they live.

A whole world of change is on its way and one that we all need to embrace. It mainly has upsides with not too many negatives. It might even save the planet!

Glossary

5G – is the new generation of cellular network infrastructure (superseding 4G) and is capable of theoretical speeds of up to 10 gigabits per second.

Active Listening – is a technique that is often used in counselling, training, and solving disputes. It requires the listener to concentrate, understand, respond and then remember what is being said.

Agile – group of software development methods that promote the development of solutions through collaboration between self-organising, cross-functional teams.

Artificial Intelligence – computer systems able to perform tasks that currently require human intelligence, for example visual perception, speech recognition, decision-making, and translation between languages.

Body Language – is a type of non-verbal communication where physical behaviors, as opposed to words, are used to convey information.

Business Intelligence (BI) Tool - this is a tool which prepares and presents data in a form which helps decision makers to make more effective data-driven decisions.

Chat Board – is an online discussion area where people with similar interests discuss topics. The contents of these discussions are usually available to be searched.

Collaboration and Coordination Software – one or a number of software packages that facilitate remote teams collaborating, communicating and sharing information, together with software that allows a manager to control and coordinate that team.

Collaboration software – Collaborative software or groupware is application software designed to help people involved in a common task to achieve their goals.

Content Sharing – refers to sharing the contents of an individual window or the whole screen in a videoconferencing package.

Cyberbullying - is a form of bullying or harassment using electronic means, also commonly referred to as online bullying.

Employee Assistance Program (EAP) is intended to help employees deal with personal problems that might adversely impact their work performance, health and well-being

Gantt Chart – a representation of a project plan in a bar chart, as promoted by Henry Gantt in the early 20th century.

Hosted Service – where a supplier of an application hosts that application on their own or a third party's servers and charges typically by use.

Instant Messaging – is the exchange of near real-time messages through a software application.

Kanban Boards - is an agile tool used to help visualize work. Kanban boards use cards, columns and continuous improvement to help Agile teams commit to work, and get it done.

Nonviolent communication (NVC) - is a way of removing the negative and adversarial elements from conversation to achieve a better result.

On-premise – software is installed and runs on computers and servers installed in the organisation's offices, rather than in the cloud.

Organisation Chart – (often called an org chart) is a diagram that shows the structure of an organisation and the relationships and relative ranks of the people shown in that chart.

Project and Task Management Software – an application typically delivered as a service over the internet which facilitates the management of geographically dispersed teams.

Project Plan – visual aid showing the tasks and resources required to complete a project, typically a plan is represented as a Gantt chart and produced using Project Management Software.

QR Code – Quick Response Code is a type of two-dimensional barcode initially developed for use by the Japanese car industry. They are now used much more widely and in a similar way to standard bar codes to identify properties of the item they are attached to or associated with.

SSO (Single Sign On) – allows a user to log on to multiple independent software systems with a single username and password.

Town Hall – a meeting where all of a company's staff are brought together, sometimes referred to as an 'all-staff meeting'.

Two-Factor Authentication – an additional level of security where a user is asked to provide a second level of validation after they've entered their username and password. This varies from being asked to quote a memorable phrase or word to keying a code produced by a hardware device.

VDI – Virtual desktop infrastructure (VDI) is virtualisation technology that hosts a desktop operating system on a centralised server in a data centre or in the cloud.

Videoconferencing – is a technology that allows users in different locations to hold face-to-face meetings without having to physically move to a single location.

VPN – A Virtual Private Network can be viewed as a secure encrypted pipe running on the public internet through which you can channel some or all data transmitted between one point e.g. a laptop computer and another (likely to be a server)

Wall of Fame – a set of images of people on a team, together with information about themselves such as interests and hobbies.

Waterfall – method of project delivery where each stage 'flows' into the next, usually comprising requirements, design, build and test stages.

Webinar – a seminar that takes place over the internet, typically using either specific Webinar software or a videoconferencing package.

Index

accents, 75

actions, 74, 122, 124

Active Listening, 61, 162

Agile, 51, 106, 162, 163

API, 122

Artificial Intelligence, 75, 162

audio-only, 58

auto-scheduling, 119, 120

back-up, 132, 133, 145

best of breed, 85, 87, 130

body language, 49, 55, 57, 58, 74, 88

capture time, 121

cloud, 97, 105, 107, 114, 130, 131, 133, 141, 143, 144, 145, 163

collaboration, 84, 85, 94, 96, 97, 98, 105, 106, 126, 130, 131, 162

communication, 49, 54, 55, 56, 57, 60, 62, 63, 66, 70, 71, 74, 76, 88, 94, 97, 103, **146**, 162, 163

Communication, **54**

communications technology, 54

constraints, 117

cultural norms, 77

daily meetings, 51

dashboard, 124

dependencies, 116, 117, 118

different cultures, 69, 70

Disaster recovery, 133

discrimination, 155

disembodied voice, 49

e-mail, 74, 84, 85, 87, 98, 113, 120, 126, 142, 144

Employee Assistance Program, 154

encryption, 114, 131, 146

encryption of data in transit, 114

encryption of your data at rest, 114

Enterprise Level Tools, 106, 107, 122

executive level view, 103

face-to-face, 56, 58, 60, 66, 164

Free trials, 127

Gantt chart, 116, 121, 164

geographically dispersed team, 96

geographically dispersed teams, 44, 84, 90, 164

geographically distributed team, 54

Google, 85, 94, 96, 124, 130

health and safety, 154

hierarchies, 73

home working, 152, 154

hosted, 89, 97, 100, 105, 108, 113

humour, 66

instant messaging, 79, 84, 85, 87, 95, 96, 97, 99, 100, 103, 126

intercultural expertise, 69

issues, 25, 51, 68, 73, 74, 75, 78, 89, 95, 96, 107, 122, 128, 153

language, 43, 55, 58, 66, 70, 75, 76, 79, 98

legal, 79, 80, 152, 154, 156

life-alienating conversation, 64

LinkedIn, 77

loneliness, 20, 21

Microsoft, 85, 94, 96, 102, 107, 124, 130

multi-factor authentication, 132

Non-verbal communication, 56

non-verbal feedback, 55, 74

Nonviolent Communication, 62, 65, 172

NVC, 62, 63, 64, 65, 163

On va lécher les vitrines, 76

on-boarding, 127

on-premise, 100, 105

Open or closed questions, 65

organisation, 20, 77, 163

Organisation Chart, 77, 163

password protected group chats, 97

personal life, 154

Phishing, 115, 144

Portfolio management, 125

portfolio view, 119

presenteeism, 72

pricing, 107, 127

profanity, 76

project based service company, 104

project delivery, 165

project management package, 84, 95, 107, 108, 115, 120, 125, 126

project management software, 84, 102, 111, 120, 125

project management tools, 104, 106, 130

project portfolio, 104, 121, 125, 126

public areas, 141

Public holidays, 80

QR, 145, 164

Quality, 92

recording, 90, 91, 107, 109, 147

relational database, 103, 107, 121, 125

reminders, 98, 120, 124

remote project manager, 1, 50, 60

reporting, 93, 107, 120, 121, 125, 126

revenue and profit, 104

risks, 104, 107, 122, 124, 140

screen sharing, 90, 147

security, 24, 99, 100, 114, 115, 125, 131, 140, 141, 142, 143, 145, 146, 164

senior managers, 73, 77

share workspaces, 130

Single Sign On, 131, 145, 164

slang, 76

small talk, 43

smart camera, 88

social routines, 74

Standard Project Management Tools, 106, 107

storage, 84, 85, 97, 113, 124, 130, 131, 133, 141, 143

stress, 20, 25, 88, 154

subscription based, 105, 108

team spirit, 74

The High End Project Management Tools, 107

The Low End Tools, 106

Time zones, 79

Training, 126

translation, 75, 79, 98, 162

user guides, 126, 127

videoconferencing, 75, 84, 85, 87, 88, 89, 90, 91, 92, 93, 94, 95, 99, 100, 130, 142, 146, 147, 163, 165

videos, 97, 127, 145

voice-only, 60, 91

VPN, 99, 141, 142, 143, 164

Wall of Fame, 43, 165

Waterfall, 165

Web chat buttons, 95

webinar, 90

WhatsApp, 95

whiteboards, 90

working hours, 79

working week, 80

YouTube, 76

Credits/Notes

[1] Flexible: friend or foe? – by Vodafone 8 Feb 2016

[2] Dell *really* wants you to work from home ... if you want - by Jeanne Sahad CNN Money June 9 2016

[3,5] The Psychology of Interpersonal Behaviour – Michael Argyle

[4] When Italians Chat, Hands and Fingers Do the Talking - Rachel Donadio – New York Times June 30, 2013

[6] Nonviolent Communication - Marshall B. Rosenberg, Ph D.

[7] The Difference: How the Power of Diversity Creates Better Groups, Firms, Schools, and Societies by Scott E. Page

[8] Want to understand accented speakers better? Practice, practice, practice. Melissa Michaud Baese-Berk, Associate Professor of Linguistics, University of Oregon The Conversation April 3, 2019

[9] Sapiens A Brief History of Humankind – Yuval Nosh Harari - Vintage 2011

[10] Epson EcoTank survey - One can be the loneliest number — many UK freelancers feel lonely and isolated following leap to self-employment. Epsom 4-9-2018

[11] Body Language; Around the World - Nuria Nakajima 30 March 2016 LinkedIn Pulse

[12] Cultural Context Inventory - Claire B. Halverson (1993)

[13] Effective Multicultural Teams: Theory and Practice (Advances in Group Decision and Negotiation) Halverson and Tirmizi 22 Jun 2008

[14] Working anytime, anywhere - The effects on the world of work International Labour Organisation and the European Foundation for the improvement of Living and Working Conditions – 2017

[15] How deep will downturns in rich countries be? Economist April 16th 2020

[16] Does working from home work? Evidence from a Chinese experiment - national bureau of economic research - Working Paper 18871 March 2013

[17] Sit less and move more to reduce risk of early death, study says. Nicola Davis - The Guardian Health 14 Jan 2019

[18] The Definitive Book of Body Language - Barbara and Allan Pease 1978

[19] The reason Zoom calls drain your energy By Manyu Jiang 22nd April 2020 BBC Remote Control

[20] Quiet The Mind – Matthew Johnstone - Robinson 5th April 2012

An acknowledged expert in project management, Gren Gale has dedicated his working life to managing projects of all sizes effectively and efficiently.

Over the last 15 years he has successfully managed projects across all five continents and gained an unrivalled expertise in what it takes to make running a project remotely work.

Founder and CEO of PM Results, a company set up to enable businesses to implement world class project management practices, he is a Prince 2 practitioner and professional Scrum Master.

For more information visit **PMresults.co.uk**

www.ingramcontent.com/pod-product-compliance
Lightning Source LLC
Chambersburg PA
CBHW052355220526
45465CB00003BA/1118